Unfinished Business

Children and the Churches

Consultative Group on Ministry among Children

D1331831

CCBI Publications
Inter-Church House
35-41 Lower Marsh
London SE1 7RL

ISBN 0 85169 253 4

Published by
CCBI Publications
Inter-Church House
35-41 Lower Marsh
London SE1 7RL

Cover Design by Alison Downie

Printed by
Design & Print
Rowan Close
Portslade
Brighton
E Sussex BN41 2PT

CONTENTS

FOREWORD

God, who in Jesus became vulnerable as a child, calls us to listen to voices which are not heard and to stand alongside those who have no position or power. Among the most vulnerable members of any society are children as their powerlessness leaves them open to exploitation. At the same time as listening and standing alongside children, we must celebrate with them as they enrich life by what they bring to it.

If we are to do these things, we must exercise our imagination to see what it feels like to be a child today in various circumstances. The world and the churches have changed in significant ways since any adult was a child. Both the benefits and the threats have increased to children who live at the end of the twentieth century and the beginning of the twenty-first.

Unfinished Business: Children and the Churches raises some important issues for the churches at local and national level. The *Child in the Church* report encouraged the integration of children into the life and worship of the Christian community for the good of both the child and the Church. There is *unfinished business* because there are still elements of that first report which we have failed to take seriously. What children bring to the life of a Christian community is still undervalued. Nurture is still often limited to offering information about the faith rather than experience of it. *Unfinished Business* encourages us to think further about children within the life of the churches.

As its title suggests, it goes beyond that to ask questions about the churches and children in society. Are we called to be advocates for children? What kind of communities do we need to be to fulfill our mission as children and adults together? *Unfinished Business* offers us insights and models of ways of working. In times past, individual Christians and churches have been prominent in defending children from abuses and in creating opportunities for a physically, emotionally, spiritually and intellectually healthy growth. Many children in Britain and Ireland, and the rest of the world, still need to be protected and to be given opportunity.

In commending the report, *Unfinished Business*, we pray that it will encourage us to act in the churches and in society alongside and on behalf of children.

Rev Hugh Davidson

Mrs Gillian Kingston

Mrs Myriel Davies

Rev Io Smith

Most Rev John Habgood

Cardinal Thomas Winning

Presidents of the Council of Churches for Britain and Ireland

The Working Group

In 1976 a working party established by the Consultative Group on Ministry among Children (CGMC) of the British Council of Churches produced the report *The Child in the Church*. This report, together with the subsequent *Understanding Christian Nurture* (1981) had a profound influence on the life and work of the churches.

In 1991 the CGMC, now a Network of the Council of Churches for Britain and Ireland, appointed a working group to consider children and the churches in the light of *The Child in the Church* and the subsequent developments in the churches, society, education and our understanding of the process of nurture.

Members of the working group are:

Vernon Blyth*	Adviser in Religious Education, Diocese of Bath & Wells
David Gamble*	Children's Work Secretary, Methodist Church Division of Education and Youth; Moderator of CGMC
David G Hamilton*	Assistant Director, Board of Parish Education, Church of Scotland
Ivor Hughes*	National Children's Officer, Church of England Board of Education
Hugh James	Vicar of Llanfihangel-ar-Arth; formerly Provincial Officer for Youth and Children's Work, Church in Wales
Houston McKelvey*	Secretary, Church of Ireland General Synod Board of Education (N. Ireland)
Margaret Old	formerly Head of Education in Churches, Scripture Union (England & Wales)
Stephen Orchard*	Director, Christian Education Movement
Simon Oxley*	County Ecumenical Officer for Greater Manchester; formerly (Convener) General Secretary, National Christian Education Council; past Moderator of CGMC
Janet Scott	Head of Religious Studies Department, Homerton College, Cambridge
David Tennant*	Head of Church Education Department, Westhill College, Birmingham

* denotes member of CGMC at date of publication

The working group is particularly grateful to Jon Doble (Barnardos), Judith Everington (Warwick University), Susan Hector (Westminster College, Oxford), Richard Hughes (formerly Diocesan Director of Education, Salisbury Diocese), John Hull (Birmingham University), Lesley Husselbee (United Reformed Church) and Paul Murray (Newman College, Birmingham) for their input at various stages of the group's work. We are also grateful to Deborah Harrison and Paula Douglas and to John Nankivell for reflecting with us on belonging to black majority and Orthodox faith communities respectively. Members of CGMC have assisted us by discussing some papers produced by the working group. We have also been informed by our personal contacts and experiences across Britain and Ireland.

The working group acknowledges the financial support of the Jerusalem Trust, the Methodist Church Division of Education and Youth and the National Christian Education Council.

The working group has been assisted by holding residential meetings at Westhill College, Birmingham.

The working group is grateful to Pamela Egan for her editorial work in preparing this document for publication.

INTRODUCTION

A group of children sit idly on the church wall. The churchgoers, as they walk past to worship, eye them warily. Are they more likely to be concerned about the fate of their cars parked vulnerably in the church car park than about the fate of those children living vulnerably in society?

0.1 This report explores the relationship between children and the churches - those children who would count themselves as part of the Church community and the vast majority who effectively have no contact with the Church.

0.2 Genuine feelings of concern are expressed in the face of examples of inhuman treatment of children, perceptions of a decline in standards of behaviour and morality and the statistics of declining numbers of children actively involved in the life of the Church. In spite of all the words, reports and resolutions and of the prompting of many agencies, groups and individuals, the churches have not yet wholly been transformed into ' child-friendly' places - either within their own life or as advocates for children in society.

0.3 The purpose of this report is not limited to an exploration of the status of children (baptized or as yet unbaptized) in the Church. The claims of all children on the churches of Britain and Ireland rest not on any particular status they may have but on the fact that they are persons. As such they have a share in God's love for all people, expressed in Jesus Christ. Children are persons who are vulnerable and to whom the structures of society and the churches give little voice. This adds to the demand that, in faithfulness to the call to be God's people, the churches must work in love not only for but with children.

0.4 The Consultative Group on Ministry among Children (CGMC) of the Council of Churches for Britain and Ireland brings together representatives of over twenty denominations and Christian organizations. In setting up the process which led to the writing of this report, CGMC believes that the time is right for the churches to re-examine their relationship with all children.

0.5 CGMC was the guiding influence behind the first ecumenical publication on children by the churches in Britain and Ireland, in 1976. *The Child in the Church* is one of the most significant reports produced by the churches and its influence is still being felt in their work. It was the outcome of a period of substantial and formative exploration of experiential approaches to Christian

1

education and the communication of the Christian faith. The role of the Sunday School was questioned and the scope of church-related education was reviewed.

0.6 *The Child in the Church* led to important distinctions being expressed between nurture, education, indoctrination and training. This debate raised such issues as:

Can Christian nurture take place without the child being accepted as a Christian?

Can Christian education be open enough to avoid the nurture process becoming at best socialization into a religious community or, at worst, indoctrination?

In response to these specific issues a second report, *Understanding Christian Nurture*, was published in 1981. This considered the theological basis for Christian education together with Christian childhood, nurture, worship and Christian parenting.

0.7 Subsequently CGMC has examined the place of the Bible in Christian education in *The Bible and Children* (1988) and children's participation in eucharistic worship in *Children and Holy Communion* (1989). CGMC also worked on the issue of child abuse with the National Children's Bureau to produce the *Taking Care* pack (1991). Most recently CGMC has produced *Kaleidoscope* (1993), training material for those who work with children in the Church. This is a piece of work significant for its methodology and breadth of church involvement and has received an enthusiastic reception. All this has complemented the work done denominationally, some of which has had a wider ecumenical influence, for instance the Church of England's *Children in the Way* report (1988) and the United Reformed Church's *Children's Charter*.

0.8 Since the publication of *The Child in the Church*, great changes have taken place in the lives of children, in the world in which they grow up, in the understanding of how faith develops and in the churches. These are outlined in subsequent chapters. This does not mean abandoning the central assertions of *The Child in the Church*; it means that new ones need to be added and others re-focused.

0.9 This report is not offered as a detailed blueprint for the churches of Britain and Ireland but as a means by which they will be helped to respond appropriately both at the local and the national level. There are no universally applicable methods but there are ways of working which are grounded in the gospel, responsive to the reality of children's lives and, through the work of the Holy Spirit, dynamic in their implications.

0.10 In the end, our relationship with God is judged on how we deal with ourselves and with other people. The motivation for Christians to care about children, however, is not the fear of judgement but a sharing in the positive delight of God in creating people to live together in community, and in particular those people we call children.

0.11 The report provides both an audit and an incentive for the churches to:

> explore what it means to be a child in today's world,
>
> promote the place of children in their life and worship,
>
> and act on behalf of all children as an advocate for them.

The child is a gift of God and a sign of the kingdom.

1   INFLUENCES ON CHILDREN TODAY

The Erosion of Childhood

1.1   Children living in Britain and Ireland in the 1990s are part of a world community. They are also part of an open society in which the generations interact more closely together. Children have readier access to the world of adults than was the case until recently. In fashion, in monetary spending power (and therefore in becoming targets for commercial enterprise), in social habits, in speech, in the home and in leisure activity, children share much of contemporary adult culture. Our society is increasingly aware of the blurring of the concepts of childhood and adulthood. Regrets are expressed that our children `are growing up too quickly' and are `being deprived of their childhood'. Some commentators conclude that the age of childhood - as a period in the human cycle characterized by innocence, play and learning - has shrunk to a span of only a few years. From halfway through the years of primary school the young person today enters the phase of the *adult-child.*

This is a period of great ambiguity and tension and a period in which society gives conflicting signals. Children may watch the same television programmes as adults and be exposed to the same world news coverage, often centred on wars, violence and human deprivation. They may be exposed through advertising to the relentless pressure of consumerism. Their attitudes cannot help but be influenced by our society's continuing preoccupation with sex. At the same time they are expected not to be anxious, not to be materialistic or possessive and not to be sexually active. The incidence of juvenile vandalism, disorder and crime and the degree to which older children and younger teenagers are caught up in antisocial and self-destructive behaviour is well documented. This is the world of the *adult-child.* Public concern and consequent Government action over so-called video `nasties' or computer pornography is indicative of trends.

1.2   The impact of television on the development of children deserves special attention, not only as a key instrument in bringing about the erosion of childhood but in fostering a social revolution which has affected the course of human development. Students of both social history and media studies have charted the rise of literacy in the general population, beginning in the Renaissance period and continuing into the early years of the twentieth century. The

4

availability of literature on a massive scale, following the invention of the printing press, led directly to the need for people to learn to read. This in turn extended the need for schooling and the consequent prolongation of childhood, giving rise to the systems of education that are our inheritance. Indeed some would say it was this phenomenon more than any other that gave rise to the expansion of childhood into the major stage of human development it is today. This notion equates adulthood with the ability to read. Children were learners and `apprentice adults'. This movement, reaching its culmination in the nineteenth century, had profound effects upon the way society was ordered and, of course, this held implications for organized religion, as is evidenced in the history of the Sunday School movement. In the first two decades of the present century the place of the child, the role of the child, the expectations of the child and the limitations of the child were relatively well-defined. All this was soon to change.

1.3 Furthermore the ready availability of the printed word advanced conceptual thought. The age of literacy has been described as the *propositional age*. Before then popular communication had been mainly through imagery. This was certainly true in the Church, as is attested in the liturgy, art and symbolism of medieval Christianity. The movement from image to word brought about a new world and, through the Reformation, new churches. All this was to change in the twentieth century when, following the electronic revolution, the image once again ruled supreme. People today watch (rather than read or listen to) television. The image is all-important. The consequences of this shift from *propositional* to *representational* thinking cannot be overestimated. This is particularly true as regards the development of children. Through the television screen they are exposed to the adult world in its entirety with the subsequent loss of `secrecy' and the erosion of childhood. Perhaps, in the longer term, it will be this re-emergence, in a more powerful way than ever, of the power of the image that will prove most problematic. The pity is that it should tend towards superficiality and trivialization. The quick fix of the sound bite, with its simplistic message, is a perverse influence in society. Whichever way we look at it, with the decline in literacy may come a decline in the capacity for reasoning. That must affect children and adults in our society and how they perceive and respond to the Gospel.

1.4 It is through play that children integrate the world of their imagination with the world experienced through the senses. The erosion of childhood is threatening to destroy children's capacity to make sense of the world in that necessary mingling of fantasy and reality which constitutes play.

It may appear on the surface that this mingling of fantasy and reality is exactly what television and the media are able to achieve. However, their power to manipulate, the influence of the passive, highly individualized activity of watching, the impact of the immediate and the simplistic and the view that if you see something then that is how it must be, create a dangerous kind of fantasy world. The consequences are a demystifying of reality and the promotion of the delusion that the world is one great theme park. Computer games channel the child's imagination in particular ways. They have a potential to develop the imagination but where they isolate children, or encourage violence, they are a cause for concern. There is a need for children to develop serious and rigorous critical thought. This will only happen if space and freedom are given in childhood for children to exercise their imaginations in play.

It is in play that children wrestle with the mysteries of life and death - as when in a game the child says to her friend `go dead' and, minutes later, `come alive now'. On many occasions children must work over problems unvoiced and dimly perceived; in the mingling of fantasy with reality an intense inner life can be externalized in play activities. By a proper regard for the development of imagination through play it becomes easier for children to control their behaviour and accept the limitations of the real world. Play is not trivial but highly serious.

1.5 As children grow they also seek for meaning by asking questions. Their queries arise from their experience and investigation of the world around them. Children must be enabled to exercise those innate capacities to explore, to relate to others, to reveal the depth and intensity of their emotional life and distinctive modes of thinking.

Changes in Family Life

1.6 Patterns of family life in the United Kingdom and Ireland are changing. More and more people live alone - more than a quarter of all U.K. households are one-person households, double the proportion in 1961. Whilst in the Republic of Ireland divorce is not available, the U.K. has one of the highest marriage and divorce rates in Europe. A quarter of all divorces involve a person who has been divorced before.

1.7 Although there has been an increase in births outside marriage, three-quarters of these births are registered by both parents and half have parents living at the same address. Only a few single women now marry between discovery of a pregnancy and the birth of the baby. The percentage of the U.K.'s population living in so-called `traditional' family units - married parents with dependent children - has declined from 52% in 1961 to 40% in 1992.

1.8 If the divorce rate in the U.K. remains at its current level almost one child in four will experience divorce in their families before reaching the age of sixteen. No formal record is made of the children of re-marrying parents, so the numbers of children who gain a step-parent are unknown. It is estimated that by 2000 only half of all children will spend their childhood with both natural parents. Although there is no divorce in the Republic of Ireland, yet there is separation and many children live with this pain.

1.9 Changes in family life mean that people are living openly in a greater variety of relationships. The range includes single parents, serial monogamous relationships and four-parent families where children encounter their parents' several families and also children from previous or consequent relationships.

1.10 One of the greatest changes in child care is that many parents today choose to pursue a career and make arrangements for others to share in looking after their children. Changing patterns of employment have led to changing patterns of family life.

Religious and Cultural Pluralism

1.11 Surveys of public opinion in Britain and Ireland consistently show a significant level of belief in God. This is despite a serious decline in levels of attendance at public worship in all Christian traditions. There is still a readiness to pray, particularly at times of personal difficulty. Most funerals are conducted in a religious context. A small but significant minority of people report experiences which they categorize as religious but which are outside the practice of any faith. These examples may be interpreted as the lingering memory of religious tradition. However, they may equally be signs that the rumour of God in people's lives has not been silenced.

1.12 Surveys cannot fully reflect the fact that Britain is a more plural society than ever before. The increase in pluralism is not always perceived to be an enriching experience and in some areas it has resulted in more tribal alignments. There is less optimism today that the U.K. is evolving into a genuinely multi-racial, pluralistic, society. There is, nevertheless, a greater awareness of different interpretations of religious experience. Racial and cultural changes have brought to Britain different religions and varieties of expressions of Christianity, some of which are closely related to national and ethnic groups.

1.13 Many children live in two cultures at the same time, speaking two different languages, one at school and another at home. For some the language of every day will be that of shops, television, papers and peer groups at school, whereas the language of religion may well be used only in the place of worship, the ceremonies and activities of the faith community and possibly the home. The rise of `Saturday Schools' and `culture classes', often based in church premises, in the case of some Afro-Caribbean and South Asian communities, or in the mosque, temple or synagogue, will contribute to educational and religious development where language is the key issue. Particular influences operate in areas where bilingualism is common, such as in Wales. Sensitivity is essential in communities where a language may be used only by a dying generation. Similarly, sensitivity is required in areas where a language is living but its use may exclude newcomers. Language and culture are directly related; the safeguard and protection of one may be necessary for the other.

Urban and Rural Contexts

1.14 Different and drastic changes are affecting both urban and rural societies, but on some issues there is commonality in the effect they can have on children. Deprivation of children occurs in all communities, although for different reasons. The development of many city centres and urban areas has taken the form of high rise buildings including high concentrations of residential accommodation. Children's needs have not been a priority. Outer suburbs may include large affluent developments of expensive housing but with few community buildings except churches and schools. Other outer suburban areas are municipal housing estates with a similar lack of provision. Some new towns are mixtures of municipal and private housing modelled on `villages'. Ethnic minority populations have occupied the older areas of many cities. Old houses may be damp, decaying and rat- or bug-ridden. Houses on new estates may be shoddily built. Play space in all areas can be limited. Crime, danger on the streets, cars and busy roads make life difficult for many children. Parental fear of these dangers leads to further restrictions on children's activities.

Many village communities also suffer from inadequate old housing alongside newer, possibly expensive housing and `conversions' of old properties. Some communities are isolated with no facilities for children: neither physical space nor activities, nor organizations, possibly no school. Many rural children must travel to the next village or even the nearest town for leisure and recreation. Streets may be badly lit, roads narrow, cars a problem, pavements and play areas non-existent. It could be said that whereas urban redevelopment is planned around the car, the village is not. Both situations deprive and threaten children.

1.15 Although rural children are often more relaxed than their urban counterparts, their small community may nevertheless not be child-friendly because it gives them little opportunity to mix with other children. They have the privilege of seeing fields, woods and open spaces and of breathing fresh air, yet the fields and woods may be private and forbidden to them. When children are a small minority in a community, questions of leadership are acute. Older people may be farming and have too much to do to take on children's work. The owner occupiers may be retired and although perhaps they offer leadership in the community it may not be for children's work. The younger people may only reside in the village but commute to work elsewhere, leaving them with little time for local involvement. Children may have to `leave' their community at an early age because schools or Cubs or Brownies are located in another village or town, and that is where their personal friendships are made. Some children live on isolated farms. This means dependence on parents and the car.

1.16 The urban child also may be forced to grow up too quickly because of lack of play facilities and space (play areas having been forced to close through vandalism), the danger of accidents on the roads, overcrowding and the difficulty of meeting others in high rise tower blocks. Leadership may be lacking in the inner urban areas because people with skills do not live there. Schools may be near at hand but often have a high proportion of probationer teachers and rapid turnover of staff. High levels of material provision raise expectations and without parental support and care can condition children to have desires which cannot be met except by theft. Boredom can lead to insecurity within families and communities in both rural and urban areas and can result in vandalism and petty crimes. Like many rural children, urban and suburban children will be dependent on parents and the car.

1.17 Children experience deprivation in many ways. The community in which they live may be run down and lack facilities. Within their homes they may be deprived of the things which matter most - love, security, encouragement - even if they appear to be well provided for in material terms. Material provision may be offered as a substitute for parental attention, or in an attempt to make up for unhappiness caused by instability in parental relationships. Frequently parents spend long hours at work away from their families in order to provide for their material needs.

Deprivation can take various forms and exists in all sections of society. For many children, however, it is exacerbated by poverty.

Child Poverty and Deprivation

1.18 Between 1979 and 1993 the proportion of children in Britain living in families receiving below 50% of average income increased from 1 in 10 to nearly 1 in 3. A study of the effects of tax and Social Security changes between 1979 and 1991/2 suggests that while there was an increase in average real income for all households, the top 10% were 62% richer after housing costs whilst the bottom 10% were 17% poorer.

Throughout Britain and Ireland the economic factor that has had most impact on children in the 1990s has been the unprecedentedly high level of unemployment. The overall trend throughout Europe for decades has been a decrease in the availability of full-time employment. This follows from technological and economic changes. The overall trend, however, masks the impact of unemployment on particular communities where, for example, the closure of a mine or shipyard causes a collapse of the local economy. In some urban areas high levels of unemployment are concentrated in a small neighbourhood perhaps of only a few streets.

1.19 Thousands more children have become temporarily or permanently homeless. Rents have increased faster than general inflation;

arrears, mortgage debts and repossessions have all increased. In England 79% of homeless households in priority need in 1990 included dependent children and/or pregnant women. One third of homeless young people are thought to be in London. Shelter estimated that over 150,000 young people experience homelessness each year as a result of leaving home or care and being unable to find or afford accommodation. The well-publicized homelessness of major cities should not mask the pain in rural areas in all parts of Britain and Ireland.

1.20 The issue of child abuse has received increased public attention. At 31 March 1993 there were 32,500 children on Child Protection Registers in England. Thirty-seven per cent of these children had suffered physical injury, while 26% had been sexually abused. The remainder had experienced neglect or emotional abuse. The majority of children on the Registers (68% in 1992) were under ten. There are no simple answers to these problems. Increasing residential provision for children is costly and not necessarily effective. Expert opinion is divided and ambivalent on the merit of taking children away from their families. There is very little provision to support families where relationships are under great stress.

1.21 Perhaps the most important conclusion to be drawn is that there is a need to develop better mechanisms than currently exist for monitoring the position of children in Britain and Ireland. The NCH Action for Children's `Fact File' produced annually, *Children in Danger*, from which the above statistics are taken, is an approach to this; as is the National Children's Bureau 1987 Report on Child Health, *Investing in the Future*. The news that with the help of Office of Population Censuses and Surveys, the Central Health Monitoring Unit in the Department of Health has begun to draw together the wide variety of information available on child health is a welcome development. But the effort needs to be broadened to include all aspects of children's lives, and Britain and Ireland should produce annual Reports on these matters. In order to monitor the lives of children adequately, up-to-date information will need to be collected. In particular, it is important to know what children themselves think and feel.

Social Prejudice in Children

1.22 Against this background it is appropriate to enquire how social prejudice develops in children and how it may be countered.

There is a sense in which the social groups in society function in a tribalistic manner as evidenced in leisure pursuits, in following sport, in both majority and minority communities and particularly in deprived or socially divided communities. Within the church and other religious communities there can be found a degree of social prejudice which makes it difficult for children to grow up able to accept and welcome others who are different from themselves.

1.23 In response to such a highly complex issue the churches must avoid adopting unconsidered solutions. The considerable amount of research which has been conducted into the formation of social prejudice indicates that it is too simplistic to say that prejudice in individuals is the direct result of social conditioning. According to Frances Aboud, *Children and Prejudice* (see booklist, p. 74), explanations for the existence of prejudice fall into one of three broad categories.

Social reflection theories hold that children's prejudices reflect the social values to which they are exposed. The different values placed on various individuals or groups by the community or family of which a child is a part will be reflected in the child's prejudices. Gradual and informal learning is the process by which children acquire social values and attitudes. Accordingly, prejudice would increase with age.

Authoritarian theories explain negative attitudes in terms of the internal psychology of the child rather than social influences. The sources of prejudice lie in anger and the defence mechanisms which deal with anger. However, it is also suggested that parents who use authoritarian child-rearing practices may reinforce this tendency.

Social-cognitive development theories claim that prejudice in young children is inevitable because of their limited understanding of themselves and their world. In each stage of the child's development the form of prejudice will be different as it will arise from a new understanding of and relationship to the social world.

Each of these categories has its strengths and weaknesses in terms of how it accounts for differences in prejudice. The churches must be aware of the research which has been done on social prejudice in understanding the role of the Christian community and its educational programmes in reducing prejudice.

1.24 Children experience considerable confusion, uncertainty and conflict where they are involved in movement from one group to another or one lifestyle to another. The individual reared in the midst of prejudice has a hard road to travel toward personal liberation, openness and maturity. It is a road which the churches themselves must travel.

Children's Rights

1.25 It is clear from various international and national initiatives that the issue of children's rights, including spiritual rights, is of paramount concern, and deserves greater prominence in the churches' thinking. In the decade marked by the International Year of the Child (1979) and the passing of the Children Act in the U.K. (1989) there was a general improvement in children's rights. The UN Convention on the Rights of the Child was adopted in 1989, building on previous legislation of 1948 and 1959.

1.26 What is a right? A right is a justifiable or proper claim to have something or to act in a certain way. A distinction needs to be made between rights of entitlement and rights of action. An important touchstone of such rights is the ability to choose. The exercise of the right to choose a particular line of action is different from choosing to receive what is on offer. So, a right of action might be to worship as we please and a right of entitlement might be to receive a particular kind of religious education. Children's rights are of both kinds and carry with them the right of waiver, especially in the context of the rights and obligations of parents and those working *in loco parentis*. The challenge as to which rights take priority over others is complex and fundamentally a moral challenge. But normally considerations about the universality of rights, the question of what is of paramount importance and what is practicable as distinct from rhetorical would certainly have to be considered.

1.27 A valuable definition of spiritual rights was originally given by John Bradford in *The Spiritual Rights of the Child* (The Children's Society). A `spiritual' right refers to the freedom of being attuned to and in rapport with the spiritual dimension of life and that process which encourages and develops it: nurture, education and not indoctrination. It is not necessarily limited to religion, it has to do with the transcendent, values which arise from that, regard for the ultimate realities of life, experiences of wonder, the capacity for joy and sadness, a sense of relatedness, the numinous, enlightenment, and the freedom to examine, be critical about, and decide about these in terms of commitments.

The spiritual rights of the child may be described as:

♦A right of the child to the best of the spiritual heritage of the culture in which the child is born.

♦A right of the child to express his or her spiritual beliefs in private and or public without discrimination.

♦A right of the child to deepen, doubt, alter or be critical of the spiritual commitment in which he/she is born and brought up.

♦A right of the child to education, family, and other institutional support, complementary to his or her spiritual development.

♦A right of the child to protection from spiritual damage and handicap as is reasonable and appropriate.

Thus the child has the right of spiritual *initiation, expression, choice, support and protection* in his/her personal growth and becoming. For example, it is known that some children are exploited for the gain of adults in pornography and prostitution. Many more are employed at hours, or for a length of time, that are illegal. Such children are being denied either access to full-time education, or protection, or both. Some parents and faith communities inhibit spiritual development by improperly imposing beliefs and values.

2 CHALLENGES TO THE CHURCH

The Church as Advocate for Children

2.1 The churches in Britain and Ireland are part of a world Church. Their witness within and to the wider community concerning the needs of children presents a major challenge. It is the Church's responsibility to be foremost in advocacy on matters affecting children, their status and welfare within society. How a church esteems its children is an index of faithfulness and health.

2.2 In response to the implications of the incarnation of Jesus Christ, the churches have an unavoidable duty to attempt to be in touch with the experiences and lives of children today. Primarily, the churches must set an example of listening to children, their hopes and their fears. There are dangers everywhere for children: child abuse (within and outside the family), environmental hazards and accidents, and street crime. The churches must recognize that children are vulnerable and in need of protection, and must speak out and act on their behalf.

2.3 Children and young people are the target of a multi-billion-pound advertising and communications industry. They live in a world of commercialism, consumerism and market forces with a heady emphasis on personal gain. The churches must promote a different lifestyle and challenge these values.

2.4 Despite some acknowledgement of the multi-cultural and multi-faith society, racism, discrimination and intolerance remain widespread and endemic. Racism and discrimination are divisive and destructive forces that have an impact on children, families, communities and on the future of our society. The churches must give a lead in challenging discrimination in Church and society.

2.5 Whilst attempting to be a Christian conscience within society, the churches must also reclaim the numinous and witness to the presence and the power of God. Implicit in this is challenge to the Church to recognize how children learn, and how they learn about God. In a world of many and different beliefs it is important that children are given the opportunity to explore belief in God for themselves and what it means for them.

2.6 The churches need to address the importance of the spiritual rights of children. How is the climate created in schools for spiritual development and in churches for spiritual formation? Spiritual development and formation is multi-faceted and complex, yet the

15

churches have the task of enabling people to make meaning of life within a world view derived from and inspired by the Christian Faith. Churches must create those conditions whereby children can be open to receiving an experience of God and ready to express their response to God. This process will include factual knowledge, emotional content and interpretation.

Church, Family and Parents

2.7 The much greater variety of family types means that growing numbers of children experience different forms of parenting and family relationships. The family remains the primary source of childhood nurture but requires different and perhaps more creative methods of support. The churches can help to achieve this.

2.8 In their earliest days children discover and learn many things. Within their home and from their parents' example they get a feeling about whether the world is a good place to be, what things in life are important and whether life is meaningful. It is to be hoped that they experience security and stability, love, trust, honesty, respect and care (although sometimes, sadly, this is not the case). They may see quarrels - but they may also see forgiveness and reconciliation. They learn their own importance - and that of other people.

2.9 In the home and family context a child may experience crises, major and minor family disputes, marriage breakdown, sibling rivalry, times of separation and loss, death of a pet or a relative, and abuse. It is within the home that a child asks many important life-or- death questions. The word `Why' is often heard. From the parent(s) a child discovers whether to ask such questions and may find areas where even the adults do not know the answers. The churches must build bridges of support and help for the home and for parents.

2.10 Children begin to discover some of the building blocks with which faith grows, long before they learn to pray or read the Bible. What they learn about themselves, the world and other people during their earliest years is a basis for everything which comes later.

2.11 Children soon start to discover what things are important to their family: whether the name of God is used, and how; what is the place of faith, prayer, worship and the wider life of the Church; whether the Bible is an important book or never opened; whether stories from the Bible and the faith community are ever told; what are the special moments in the year and how they are marked; whether Christmas is just about expensive presents and excesses of food and drink - or whether it is something more. Parents need encouragement, support and even materials to help them to introduce children to the Christian faith from their earliest years.

2.12 Being a parent can be one of the most rewarding and most difficult jobs in the world. It is a stressful role and a heavy responsibility. Changing social patterns and structures create isolation and increase the burdens of parenting. New parents receive little or no preparation and training for their role and in many ways society does not seem to treat being a parent as of great significance. Especially with a first child parents worry whether they are doing things the right way, even though there is no one `right way' - each parent, child and situation is different. Later, discipline can become a problem and many parents (and teenagers) find teenage years full of hazards. The needs of both parents and children are inextricably intertwined. Finding better ways of supporting and nurturing parents must be a goal of social policy. The churches must help to achieve this nationally and locally, beginning with their own congregational and community life.

2.13 Christian parents face a particular challenge, not only to bring their children up but to bring them up in the Christian faith, reflected for many in the commitment made at their child's baptism or dedication. It is essential that the churches provide preparation and follow-up support so that Christian upbringing can take place in the home with parents playing a key role. What the local church does for its parents may be more important than what those parents do for the church. This may demand human and material resources in the provision of programmes, events and parent/family occasions for worship and recreation. It could mean simply providing opportunities to share problems and difficulties with those in similar stages of parenting in an atmosphere of trust and support. The enjoyment of family life is a good thing and churches should encourage it.

2.14 The different patterns of family types challenge the churches to look hard at their use of the word `family', and what images of belonging this conveys. The problem of `family' worship is its association in the popular mind with nuclear family units. Unconditional acceptance of single parents, four-parent families, single-sex families and unmarried or common-law parents will pose questions about marriage and divorce, and these cannot be ignored. Yet at the same time the Christian community must be inclusive. An uncritical acceptance of prevailing cultural values and patterns will be resisted, but equally a prior judgement of those outside the traditional patterns of family and marriage may be a denial of the Gospel itself. churches must take care not to exclude those without children in their over-emphasis on the idea of `family'.

Children in Church

2.15 The falling numbers of young people belonging to the churches' youth and children's groups has given great cause for concern. In most youth organizations originally established to provide for teenagers the average age has plummeted and these organizations now focus on children in the middle years of primary school. Traditional organizations such as Sunday Schools have failed signally to take account of this fundamental shift. Whatever the reasons, the range of years during which the Church may expect to influence its children has been compressed to a very few, usually too few to establish an effective programme of nurture.

2.16 One dilemma which faces the Church is the duration of `childhood'. On the one hand, there seems to be a desire to maintain childhood as the extended period of years associated with the years of infancy and schooling, with all that this involves in maintaining children's organizations within the Church. On the other hand, there is a growing wish to see congregations as whole communities of faith, with the youngest and the oldest integrated into the collective life and worship. This has given rise to the promotion of all-age or inter-generational worship and events and is linked with another general trend in society toward the promotion of the rights of children. Both in Church and society many ambiguities and tensions are in evidence which centre on the current definition of `childhood' and the assessment of the needs of children. In such a climate of uncertainty perhaps it is not surprising that the parameters and expectations of children's work have become blurred.

2.17 The demands on the Church's work with children are urgent, yet programmes, activities and organization must be placed in a clear theological framework. This means being true to the Gospel and not merely pragmatic or sentimental. It is as dangerous and misleading to idealize childhood as it is to deny it or contribute to its erosion. The churches are now a minority in a predominantly secular society with many diverse and, at times, contradictory values. To some degree this is related to an increase of religious fundamentalism. An end result for the child is perplexity about the validity of the values being communicated. This is related to the wider issue of religious identity. Do we define our faith-identity through exclusion: defining Christianity as not being Jewish or Muslim? Or do we define it through inclusion: recognizing the revelation of God through other world faiths? This issue leaves the churches with conflict, dichotomies and choices.

2.18 Churches are beginning to recognize the contribution and entitlement of children to spiritual development. This is reflected in the concern for the process of faith development within the faith community, as well as the content. Furthermore, those who share faith need to be committed to the faith journey and to its children as fellow travellers. Children seldom grow in faith where adults do not grow in faith. Where both are growing in faith children's ministry offers belonging, significance and identity. The organization of the local congregation can either enable or hinder worship and learning. For example, the `Family Church' ideas of the 1950s were perceived to be more acceptable in prosperous, suburban churches than in other churches.

2.19 There has been an enrichment in churches where there has been a re-awakening to biblical metaphors and visions of the faith community. For example, there has been a recognition that the Church has been created and shaped by the faith story which has been passed on to it and that its task is to tell that story. The story grows and is enriched as it is told and received. This is a process which helps participants know the story as their own story. It also acknowledges that all participants can be both teachers and learners, irrespective of age or mental ability. However, due recognition must be taken of the fact that sacred scripture comes as an alien form to many young people and is seen as old-fashioned and irrelevant. An essential aspect of responsible communication is to enable children to confront and wrestle with the values and relevance of the Kingdom of God in this modern age. This is not to ignore the importance of Bible-based Christian education; the necessity to be biblical is essential to all churches. What it means is more controversial.

2.20 The process of faith sharing with children presents the churches with a significant challenge over the provision and content of worship. The language of the liturgy must be such that it can convey power, beauty and meaning for people of all ages, including children. Fundamental to this process can be the annual journey through the Christian Year with its various festivals and seasons, each reflecting new insights and emphases. Liturgical changes in some churches have led to increased lay participation in the conduct of worship, and to greater emphasis on a more regular participation in Holy Communion. These changes, which emerged from liturgical emphases like the `Parish Communion' movement, and from ecumenical studies on the nature of baptism and the position of children within the covenant community of the Church, have contributed significantly towards children being permitted to receive Holy Communion in a variety of circumstances. This significant change in the churches signifies a new awareness of the role and place of children within the worship of the Church.

2.21 While it is clear that the churches are presently going through a period of experimentation and renewal of forms of worship, it is less clear how contemporary churches value ritual. There appears to be an ambivalence toward the place of ritual in the corporate life of churches which reflects a lack of appreciation of the importance and function of ritual in our society as a whole. No social group can survive without its particular patterns of ritual behaviour. From the time that a newly created group recognizes the need for social organization and seeks to develop a coherent system of expression, that group creates or appropriates symbols which, taken together, form a means of communication which through repetition, familiarity and association constitutes ritual behaviour. This is as true of the world of business, the military or of sport as it is of the religious life. The problem for the churches, as for other institutions in society, is not ritualism in itself but the adherence to symbols and rituals which are no longer appropriate, relevant or helpful. Any effective review of worship, liturgy and the sacraments and ordinances of the churches requires more than superficial tinkering with church services. It must be born of an awareness of the fundamental importance of ritual and an understanding of the nature and function of ritual processes and the symbols incorporated in them. It simply is not possible for any social organization to dispense with ritual altogether and survive.

In the religious life the most fervent anti-ritualist who seeks to purge worship of ritualism simply replaces one ritual with another. As has been noted, fundamentalists who are not magical in their attitude to the Eucharist become magical in their attitude to the Bible! It may be worthwhile recalling that ritual and liturgy are not one and the same thing but that some rituals take liturgical form. Against this background it is pertinent to ask why it is that, in religious rituals, most people today have become passive spectators. At Vatican II, Romano Guardini said: `Liturgy is not individual worship. It demands that people pray together.' Actions are important. Even watching must become seeing, looking with attention, because all the people are involved. It is worth asking whether Christian congregations are still capable of truly liturgical action. It is also important to take seriously children's developing appreciation of symbol and ritual which are so central in their experience of play and fantasy. Perhaps the churches need to pay greater heed to the power of appropriate symbols in developing and sustaining the life of faith, to act with greater confidence in purging ritual of symbols that are no longer relevant and to create and discover new symbols appropriate to our needs.

2.22 Central to the worship of most churches and denominations is the Holy Communion. Here symbol and ritual can be at their most profound and dramatic. Communication here is through the senses and feelings as well as the intellect. Participation of children in the Holy Communion can contribute both to the sense of community and of being in God's presence. The eucharistic ritual emphasizes the `root metaphor' of Christianity, the death and resurrection of Jesus. The whole environment, the music, the words spoken and the symbols used must emphasize this. The child belongs within the group and is part of the faith family, the congregation. At other occasions of religious ritual including marriage, and Christian burial, the principle remains constant - it is that of inclusion. The child belongs within the community.

Learning Together in Church

2.23 School, as a model for Christian education, has exercised a major influence on the aims, process and content of church-led programmes of education. For some children the schooling metaphor has meant that learning is something left behind when you grow up, and for some adults its association with formal and didactic methods of learning have acted as an effective roadblock to any progress along the path of religious and spiritual formation. The churches must continue to free themselves from the historical legacy of this understanding of schooling upon the Christian education and nurture of children, and channel energies and expertise to create more appropriate models of faith-sharing amongst people of different ages.

2.24 Despite many of the insights arising from excellent faith development work in church- based education in recent years, there appears in congregational life to be a continuing and fundamental lack of understanding of this work. It is apparent that many adults involved in children's ministry view their role as one of `teaching about ....' The role of `enabler' - someone who provides opportunities for children to discover for themselves - is met with reluctance because it provokes feelings of insecurity in those required to `enable'. The tendency persists for adults to replicate their own experience of Christian nurture and education. This is inevitable when they fail to fulfill the enabling role. To stress the importance of the leaders as the `role model' means that serious questions must be raised about the ability of such leaders to deliver an effective form of Christian nurture and education. Obviously leaders must be given the opportunities and the support to understand, appreciate, accept and implement such developments.

2.25 A schooling model which casts the teacher in the role of the one who knows and the pupil as the one who needs to know is neither beneficial nor appropriate in terms of church education, since all are learners in the Kingdom of Heaven. The worship activities and teaching programmes of the churches must become places of Christian learning and growth for all people, `teacher' and `learner' alike, regardless of age, gender or race.

2.26 The challenge to the churches is to present good news to children. It is not easy to motivate a child in a sequence of once a week sessions. Teaching must be balanced with experience in the community, in worship and in fellowship activities. More variety in community activities, such as picnics, workshops, camps, homes, better use of Sunday, would supplement or even replace more traditional teaching classes, and give a more holistic approach. Churches should also take account of the religious education which children experience in schools (see Chapter 3).

2.27 There is a growing awareness of the importance of ministry *with* children as distinct from ministry *to* children. This encourages children to minister within the faith community which enables their faith development. For the churches to work with integrity with children they have to create an environment within which children on their spiritual `quest' know that `it is all right to question'. The churches must continue to provide hospitable places for this human and spiritual development. This must be accompanied by considerable care in the selection and training of those leaders who exercise responsibility in this area of ministry.

2.28 Despite the fact that there appears to be a great variety of work with children in many churches, the tendency is to be involved with an ever smaller percentage of children from mainly socially privileged backgrounds. The experience of the uniformed organizations is important in this regard. The churches must face the challenge of creating, developing and nurturing congregations as faith communities which are relevant to and meaningful to the societies in which they are situated. Many churches in urban areas have died because older and probably white congregations have failed to welcome people from ethnic minority backgrounds. On the other hand many indigenous congregations in those same areas are confident, hopeful, welcoming and accepting of all, including the children, in less-structured, informal patterns. Black-led churches have their own distinctive styles of teaching, often accompanied by an exuberance and enthusiasm in worship which is all- inclusive, adults and children together.

Evangelism and Children

2.29 Faith in the God who is revealed in Jesus Christ through the Holy Spirit is expressed in personal relationship with God and with others. This is demonstrated in the welcome and acceptance of the Christian community. It is witnessed in prayer and at worship, both personal and corporate. It is told in scripture, doctrine and teaching. The Church is challenged to communicate, in the words of John Sutcliffe (in *Learning and*

Teaching Together, 1980), `such a vision of life, faith and the world as will fascinate children enough to win their allegiance to Christ. An aim of the Church will be to enable children to have experiences of faith which are such that they will both learn about it and participate freely in it.'

2.30 This raises the question of evangelism and its connection with education and nurture. Evangelism can mean forcing one's views on others. This is particularly disturbing when it happens to children. `Even those who believe in the importance of evangelism are apt to describe it as "preaching the Gospel in such a way that people are brought to belief." This on the one hand encourages pictures of standing on a soap box preaching in stylized ways with little place for listening; and on the other hand hints at putting emotional pressure on people to make them change their beliefs.' - General Synod Board of Education and Board of Mission (1991).

2.31 The `evangel' is good news; the suffix `ism' when added to it refers to the procedures, actions and systems appropriate to that. Evangelism is about the activities designed to help people discover the good news for themselves. Evangelism belongs to the Church's Mission. The Church is charged with communicating the life, death and resurrection of Jesus Christ which is God's good news. Often it involves words but not inevitably so. Identification and solidarity with people are indispensable to the task and may in many instances be the form of evangelism which elicits response to God in Christ. Music, drama, mime, symbol and sign and any form of non-verbal presentation can all be used in evangelism.

2.32 *All God's Children?* identifies five features of this understanding which would correspond well to faith development and educational insights (see also Chapter 4):

(i) It focuses on the story being told and the telling of it is `story orientated' rather than `response orientated' and for children this is important. At their stages of faith development it is right to be `investing in the future' rather than seeking an adult style conversion response.

(ii) It avoids commitment to any particular means of communication. Rather than talking of `proclaiming the gospel' - with all the associations of preaching at people - it settles for `making known the gospel'. As far as children are concerned it is important that they should, at least in part, discover the gospel for themselves through experiences and encounters rather than by verbal onslaught.

(iii) The third strength lies in its emphasis on `identification and solidarity'. This corresponds directly with Westerhoff's styles of faith - experienced and affiliative (see sections 4.3 & 4.4 below). It also indicates the importance a congregation should attach to the welcome it gives to children in the faith community.

(iv) It shows respect for the dignity and vulnerability of those being evangelized. It is all too easy to sway and manipulate children, even if unintentionally.

(v) The fifth strength - and, noticeably, it comes at the end - is `the hope that their hearers will come to faith'.

2.33 The churches need to examine the nature of religious commitment and how it is shaped and informed. In this area there is an obvious need to re-assess the insights of faith-development theorists in relation to the area of spiritual formation. In pursuing such a quest the churches have no option but to challenge those within the Christian faith and other faiths who attempt to indoctrinate others. Fundamental to this is a recognition that what is presented as `education in faith' can often indoctrinate. Like the process of education, indoctrination is complex and multi-disciplinary and may be either aim, content or method, possibly a combination of those features.

2.34 With sensitivity there is a place for presenting the good news to children, providing the dignity of children is affirmed by giving them freedom to choose without pressure and in their own way, within their own experience and ways of understanding.

3 CHILDREN, EDUCATION AND SCHOOLS

Changing Perceptions and Practices

3.1 School is a significant experience for the vast majority of children in Britain and Ireland. Only a small number of children undergo the equivalent of formal education in the home. The previous chapters have recognized the powerful influences of family and life in society on children's well-being and development. Education and school must also be taken seriously as significant experiences for children.

3.2 The education systems of Britain and Ireland have seen tremendous changes, particularly in the course of this century. A visitor to almost any primary school today is likely to see children working together in groups, engaged in different curriculum activities. A teacher might be helping a child with reading here or a group with a science experiment over there. Although today schools also use formal methods in class at certain times, fifty years ago the picture would have been quite different. Pupils sat at desks in rows throughout the day with the teacher at the front delivering the same lesson to the whole class. The contrast is not so evident in secondary schools, though here also it is true to say that students are expected to take an active part in their own learning and assessment.

3.3 This illustrates the swing towards the child-centred approach to learning which came to the forefront of educational thinking in the 1960s. Recent re-assertions of the importance of subject-based learning do not diminish the importance of experiential methods of learning and teaching. Children are not passive participants in the learning process. They bring experience and understanding of their own to their learning. They are encouraged to learn collaboratively and to take responsibility for their own learning. The child is at the heart of the process by which individuals achieve their fullest potential in academic, social or creative skills.

A Christian Approach to Education

3.4 It is generally recognized that education is an essential need. A significant proportion of governmental revenue, whether raised nationally or locally, is spent on education in the Republic of Ireland and the U.K. Yet when we come to ask what education is and what it is for, a wide variety of answers are offered. This leaves education systems and schools vulnerable to the preferences of politicians and educationists.

3.5 There is no one single Christian view of education. However, there is a number of starting points which arise out of Christian faith and are informed by the discipline and practice of contemporary education. The following offers a list of some of the key concepts (which by their nature overlap and do not fall into any logical sequence).

- ◆ **Exploration**

    A powerful image of God is of one who continually invites people to discover that which is beyond them. The great journeys of the Bible, such as the story of Abraham or the Exodus, are about making discoveries - about human relationships and about the nature of God. We may want to call our explorations by different names - science, creative art, worship. Whatever the name we use, the educational process is one of pilgrimage and discovery.

- ◆ **Community**

    The idea of community runs through the Bible - from the growing understanding of the community of the people of God in the Old Testament, through the communities of disciples and early Christians, to the community of the Kingdom of God. It is by being in community that individuals find fulfilment and achievement of their potential. Education is also for whole communities and not just for the individuals who comprise them.

- ◆ **Personal**

    The biblical witness to the personal experience of God and to the Incarnation serve as theological reminders of the importance of the individual person. A task of education is to help individuals to discover `Who I am' and `Who I am becoming'. An understanding of sin does not allow a naïve view of education as a smooth process of personal development leading to perfection. Yet, however fallible, each person is still unique and of inestimable value.

- ◆ **Relationship**

    God does not work in isolation but enters into relationship with individuals and humanity. Relationships are necessary for effective learning, promoting both   dependence and inter-dependence.

+ **Participation**

The Israelites trudging across the desert and the disciples sent out by Jesus to preach and heal are signs of participation in learning. However, simple participation in education (being there and doing things) is not enough. The two stories mentioned are powerful because they represent the results of reflection on experience. The educational process consists of reflection being brought to bear on experience.

+ **Justice**

Not the kind of justice which simply lets the punishment fit the crime or rewards according to the good done, but the puzzling, seemingly unfair justice of God which acts to put right that which is wrong and to provide for people's need. This justice is often obscured by human greed. It is much easier to run schools and society on the former view of justice. If children and communities are to be served in a Christian way, the latter understanding has to be taken seriously. To give one illustration: however generous, resource provision for schools is always finite. Does justice demand that each child has an equal share? Or does it demand that some children, for instance those with special needs or those with special gifts, be given a larger share than the others?

3.6   Taking such theological ideas as starting points may help Christians move away from a sterile debate on whether education is to fit people to the needs of society or enable them to be themselves, to memorize specific information or to discover general principles, and so on. The quartet beloved by curriculum theorists - knowledge, understanding, skills and attitudes - may be found in each of the concepts above.

3.7   Christian engagement with education cannot remain at the level of ideas. The practice of good education within the life of the Church should be the ground of a critique of education in society. churches need to provide helpful models of education, based on a Christian concept of persons created in the likeness and image of God.

Challenges to Three Common Assumptions

3.8 Rather in the way that nineteenth century philanthropists believed that poverty and crime would be eliminated once proper homes and reasonable jobs were provided for the poor, so too many believe education to be the panacea that will cure society's ills. In much thinking there is an underlying assumption that education in itself has the power to transform everything for the good. In the context of an imperfect and sinful world, however, education alone will never be able to deliver a perfect society. Certainly education can and does play a key role in changing individuals and societies for the better. Christian faith, however, proclaims the work of Christ as the perfecter of individuals and society.

3.9 Another common assumption is that education is the sole preserve and responsibility of schools and other educational institutions. Politicians and parents alike are quick to blame schools for the perceived failings of individual children and whole generations. Schools may be partly at fault, as they have sometimes given the impression that they are the only places where children's education happens. This is likely to be reinforced if education systems become more market-orientated. Schools will be seen as offering a service to the customer - who is not the child, but parents and future employers. Parents and communities (including churches) have been happy to collude with the belief that education happens only at school. The education of children is in fact the responsibility of parents, the local community and society. Schools are one means of exercising this responsibility, not a substitute for it. Learning happens, for good or ill, through the very process of living - through relationships, experiences, influences and participation.

3.10 An assumption which still needs to be challenged is that education is for children and young people alone. Invite any group of adults to reflect on what they have learnt in the past week and the result will be an amazing variety of information, skills and attitudes. Like children, adults learn in a wide variety of formal and informal ways. In spite of people's own experience, churches, in common with others, find it difficult to view education as a lifelong process which needs to be enabled. Those models of education which turn children into `finished products' as adults exercise too powerful and deceptive an influence. The greatest benefit of education is in its capacity to make us, whether as child or adult, want to continue the activity of learning throughout life.

Pre-school Provision

3.11 Young children need opportunities to play and to develop relationships. As they enjoy being themselves, the capacity for learning is developed. There is, and needs to be, a variety of provision. There is a role for *both* nursery schools and pre-school playgroups.

3.12 The churches have often been partners with statutory bodies in the provision of pre-school education. Many pre-school playgroups are based in church premises. Churches have often seen these as an opportunity to make links with families: in other words, they are seen as part of an evangelistic strategy. Even though their leaders will have an understanding of the educational value of such playgroups, they are not always seen as part of an educational strategy for the Church or in society.

3.13 Among some Christians there is a strong belief that young children should remain predominantly at home. However, there is considerable evidence that they benefit from the wider opportunities offered at playgroup or nursery school. This can be complementary to life in a loving home environment. For some young children it may be the only opportunity they have of forming relationships with caring adults.

3.14 Positive adult role models are important to a child's development. These need to be both male and female. However, the leaders or teachers in playgroups and nursery schools (infant schools, too) are almost universally women. Sensitivity to the need to protect young children from abuse should not deny them the opportunity of relating to men as leaders and teachers.

Schools

3.15 Historically the churches in Britain and Ireland were the principal providers of education. Today that historic involvement is continued and expressed in a variety of contexts through a wide range of schools and approaches to education and its management. A concern for *all* children dictates such interest and involvement and some churches' concern for their own schools at national and local levels should not be seen to exclude them from the broader debates.

3.16 The scope of the churches' involvement is wider than simply with religious education and worship (religious observance in Scotland) in schools. It will include everything which relates to and impinges upon the spiritual, moral, personal, social and creative development of children. It will involve an active concern for curriculum development, teacher training and support, and the provision of committed, informed management in order to contribute to the creation of an ethos in schools which reflects Christian values.

3.17 To maintain and further develop this contribution to the ongoing provision of positive education, the churches cannot simply rely on placing Christians on boards or committees through rights of nomination. As several churches have already recognized, it is vital that people occupying these positions (whether they are parents, clergy, teachers or other church members) possess or are equipped with the necessary skills and understandings. These include the capacity to reflect theologically on the disciplines and influences which contribute to education.

3.18 It will benefit those who exercise a ministry by serving schools in the above capacity to meet together at national, regional and local levels. This could be encouraged ecumenically.

3.19 It lies beyond the purpose of this report to make definitive statements about religious education and collective worship (religious observance in Scotland). However, churches and individual Christians need to recognize the complexity of the debate centring on this subject. For some Christians, worship cannot happen outside a community of commitment. For others, worship is an opportunity for children to experience something which lies at the heart of the practice of Christianity. Collective worship in schools was never intended to be an equivalent of what happens in churches. However well run collective worship is in schools, and in a minority it is a good and positive experience for all concerned, churches need to make their own provision for children to grow in understanding and appreciation of Christian worship. The same is largely true of religious education which, at its best, is supportive of the spiritual growth of Christian children but is not a substitute for nurture and induction within the fellowship of the Christian Church. In this report the emphasis is not so much on what the schools can do for churches as what churches can do to support children in school.

3.20 Schools should be able to look to the local community, especially the churches, for support for the values and principles which they try to embody and communicate. The attitude of churches to their local schools should be informed, sympathetic and supportive.

3.21 In the educational process within schools the role of the teacher is central. The teacher as enabler of learning as well as giver of knowledge requires a high level of professional skill and understanding of human relationships. Yet many teachers feel unsupported, under-valued and at the mercy of changing political agendas. Careful organization is essential to good learning. Administrative burdens placed on teachers, however, often appear to outweigh the demands of planning creative learning experiences for the children. Other adults, too, play an important role in the effective functioning of a school and in the children's learning. Churches should be supportive of all adults who work with children.

3.22 The churches need to affirm and encourage the vocation of teaching and other work which supports children. Christian teachers need the personal and prayerful support of their local churches for their work in school. Too often they are seen instead as a potential source of recruitment for leadership in the church's work with children.

3.23 Most schools are anxious to make links with their local community. Where this is the case, churches should be at the forefront of a response. Whether they go into the school to assist with classroom activities and specific projects (hearing readers, or research into the history of the neighbourhood) or help children from the school to be active in the community, Christian people can be in partnership with schools. However, churches must be clear about their motivation. It will be counter-productive for both church and school if churches simply see this as an opportunity to recruit children.

3.24 Honorary school chaplains in non-denominational schools have been appointed in some areas (for example, in Scotland). In addition to their pastoral work they are symbolic of the churches' concern for children, their education and the total school community. Recent experience of the provision of various forms of chaplaincy to schools and colleges, using both lay and ordained

32

people, offers a significant pointer to the way in which the work of colleges and schools can be actively supported by Christians. Such chaplaincy requires careful negotiation between school and churches. For the churches it implies an understanding of educational chaplaincy and a commitment to it in terms of support and training.

3.25 In other areas, regular visits to schools are made by ministers and clergy. A school may be visited by the minister of the parish in which it is situated or by a minister delegated by an ecumenical clergy meeting. Ministers need to accept the necessity of the school to be willing to receive such visits and to discover how, in that particular school, best use of the visit may be made. This will involve careful preparation, especially in conjunction with the staff, so that the visitor is fully aware of the school's ethos and philosophy. Such visits may be the only contact the children will have with a minister.

3.26 There is too high a price to be paid - and regrettably in some areas this is already obvious - when churches retreat from engagement in and with education. Where this has happened or is being considered, those church members who are involved become disillusioned with the institutional churches. Furthermore, the churches are by such a retreat abrogating their responsibilities under the Gospel.

3.27 The churches need to be imaginative and creative in making good use of the opportunities which already exist for involvement in the education systems. The churches have been pioneers in education. If the churches are again to give a lead to society in the provision of education which meets the needs of children and community, it will demand not only goodwill but a strategic commitment of human resources, lay and ordained, and a recovery of belief in the centrally Christian purposes of education.

4 THE CHILD AND THE COMMUNITY OF FAITH

Christian Nurture Revisited

4.1 Since the publication of *The Child in the Church* (1976) and *Understanding Christian Nurture* (1981) there have taken place a number of significant developments which have both influenced and advanced our perception of nurture in Christian faith and life. Yet the fundamentals remain the same. The Christian nurture of children is a process of planned and unplanned learning incorporating the total experience of belonging in the Christian community. This experience encompasses the variety of ways in which young people are introduced to the life and culture of the Church and are encouraged to identify with it. Nurture is the work, wittingly or often unwittingly, of the whole people of God. All that the Church is and all that it aspires to be provides the context for the experience of the individual child who comes within the domain of the Christian community. Individual experiences are influenced by particular forms of church life and by the perceptions and practice of families as they respond to the invitations of, and engage in, their local congregations. Congregations vary to a very considerable degree in their awareness of the needs of children and of the rightful place they have in the midst of the people of God. Attitudes vary, as does practice. Some congregations more than others exhibit a readiness to include children and teenagers in worship and in the community life of the group. To this extent the shaping of policy with regard to the nurture of the young and the implementation of policy differs to a bewildering extent across congregations. At best, Christian nurture focuses on the creation and provision of the most enabling conditions and opportunities for the child's development in faith, understanding, witness and service.

4.2 Horace Bushnell (1802-1876) may be said to be the forerunner of the modern Christian nurture movement. His theory of nurture was developed in reaction to the revivalist movement of his day in the United States. Whereas the revivalists emphasized the total depravity of every individual and urged people to undergo a radical conversion to faith in Jesus Christ, often orchestrating their meetings to bring about quite traumatic `conversion experiences', Bushnell adopted a more optimistic view of the human condition. In his challenge to the revivalists he maintained that in pursuing the true idea of Christian education the child should grow up a Christian and never know himself as being otherwise. In other words, the aim, effort, and expectation should be that the child would not, as was commonly assumed, grow up in sin, but in years of maturity would be open to the world as one that is spiritually renewed, not remembering the time when he or she went through a `technical' experience.

According to Bushnell, the life of the adult world, and especially of parents, flows into the children as life flows from the trunk into the branches of a tree. This is an inevitable process and it is for the adults in a Christian society, especially parents, to ensure that the nurture their children receive is Christian. From this position Bushnell argued that Christian adults had a responsibility to live lives that witness unambiguously to Christian faith. `Have it first in yourselves, then teach it as you live it; teach it by living it; for you can do it in no other manner.'

4.3   Fully a century later John Westerhoff III stands in the same tradition of a socialization approach to Christian formation. Like Bushnell, Westerhoff focuses on the importance of significant adults for the development of faith in children, but he places greater emphasis on the role and influence of the faith community as a whole. `Faith can only be nurtured within a self-conscious community of faith.' For Westerhoff the formation of Christian faith is not merely the consequence of socialization. He chooses to describe the process as `enculturation' and in so doing focuses on the interaction between gospel and culture. Westerhoff, writing for a different age and in different circumstances from Bushnell, has no difficulty with the concept of conversion per se but he views this in the context of the ongoing nurturing process.

Westerhoff has offered a highly imaginative model for understanding the means by which the individual comes to personal Christian commitment. This focuses on the congregation as the crucible of faith, witness and service. The personal growth of individuals takes place in the context of the faith community. Hence the individual's opportunities to experience faith in the lives of others, to *affiliate* to their `styles' of faith, to *question* the faith propositions and activities of the group and in due course to *own* or personalize that faith in ways unique to each individual yet recognizably informed by the group, are opportunities provided by the community of faith as a whole.

4.4 In focusing not only on the role of the home but of the congregation Westerhoff stresses the significance of liturgy in the formation of Christians and in building up the Church to achieve its mission and vocation. Liturgy is seen as the work of the Church both in its worship as the community of faith and in its daily witness as the body of Christ. From this dual activity stems the Church's engagement in mission. Because enculturation through liturgy, understood in this broad sense, is intentional and implicit in the life of the faith community, and because Westerhoff regards a schooling or institutional model to be inappropriate to personal and community development in the congregation, he adopts the term catechesis to describe the means of achieving growth.

The use of the term *catechesis* is for some Christian traditions problematic. Westerhoff offers a wide and embracing definition when he describes *catechesis* as `the process by which persons are initiated into the Christian community's faith, revelation and vocation; the process by which persons, throughout their lives, are continually transformed and formed by and in the community s living tradition.' Whether the use of the term *catechesis* helps or hinders our appreciation of the broad experience of Christian nurture is an open question. The Greek verb from which it comes, *katecheo*, stems in turn from the root *echein*, to `sound' or `ring'. The history of these words is bound up with notions of instruction and teaching and it is for precisely this reason that a recent Church of England report on an integrated approach to Christian initiation, in referring to the `catechumenal process', proposes the adoption of the term *enquirer.*

Westerhoff s concept of *catechesis* is a model of Christian nurture which embraces a number of features including home and church, worship as a learning experience (although it is rather more than that), the provision of opportunities for people to prepare for *participation* in the whole worship, life and witness of the congregation, and a process which encourages personal development through experience reflection, commitment and action. Whatever semantic confusion surrounds his notion of catechesis, it represents a rich and promising framework within which we may be encouraged to develop our ministry among children.

Learning and the Development of Faith

4.5 The last twenty years or so have seen a number of advances in the understanding of how the individual's faith develops. The extensive research project into the development of faith undertaken by James Fowler in the United States during the 1970s and 1980s has opened up a whole new field of study and debate. Fowler's earlier work culminated in the publication of *Stages of Faith* in which he identified six possible stages of faith in the human life-cycle. The discussion on the nature of these stages and of how the individual moves from one stage to another is fairly technical and draws extensively on the work of psychologists, educationists and theologians such as Erik Erikson, Jean Piaget, Laurence Kohlberg, H. Richard Niebuhr and Paul Tillich. Fowler has demonstrated convincingly that faith is by no means static but is subject to change, whether as an experience of growth or regression. The idea that faith develops through a sequence of stages somewhat like a stairway is not without its difficulties and Fowler himself has been careful not to make excessive claims but simply offers it as a working model. (An accessible introduction to Fowler's work can be found in *How Faith Grows*.)

Another academic to pursue Piaget's ideas of stage development as applied to religious and moral judgements is Fritz Oser of Switzerland. Whereas Fowler has focused more on faith development in the faith communities of the churches, Oser has concentrated on the development of religious judgment in the context of school and in the sphere of religious education. Like Fowler, Oser and his colleagues have stimulated a rich and productive discussion on religious development through the life-cycle and have prompted others to apply their findings to a range of practical concerns including those relating to Christian nurture and religious education. The American Catholic writer Gabriel Moran has brought his concern for precision of language and of analysis to bear on the work of Fowler and has expressed considerable unease over the whole conception of faith development where the impression is given of progression from lower stages to higher stages. He enquires whether the `religiously developed' consider themselves `higher' than others. He is also critical of some of the theological assumptions (such as the distinction made between faith and belief) made by Fowler and the experimental design employed in gathering data. At the same time, Moran has emphasized the desirability of lifelong learning and has defined adulthood as a *process* of maturation.

4.6 Theories of stage development such as those propounded by James Fowler and others, for all the difficulties accruing to them, have the considerable merit of emphasizing the dynamic character of faith. Faith is a process. It is subject to change and development and so is transitional in nature. Precisely how and under what conditions these transitions take place is the subject of continuing study at the present time. What is of immediate consequence is the reinforcement of the insight, if such be needed, that childhood is not a static entity, just as there is nothing fixed or final about adulthood. How individuals manage their own personal development and how they may be assisted and enabled to develop meaningfully and creatively is the concern of the related disciplines of nurture and education. Lifelong learning must become more than a slogan in the Church if individuals are to be helped in managing the transitional process in the life-cycle that brings the fulfilment and maturity that foster the realization of the Kingdom of God within them.

4.7 In addition to the interest in faith development, other areas relating to the theory and practice of Christian education have received attention in the past two decades. These might be summarized as the relationship between worship and learning; the movement away from school-based models and toward liturgical and all-age (i.e. inter-generational) models; the greater appreciation of the catechetical and nurturing responsibilities of the faith community and the role of the community as educator; the growing awareness of the spiritual insights and capacities of children; the significance of task-orientated learning and action/reflection ways of learning in faith and, in some denominations, the place of the liturgy as the context for nurture.

From this activity among theorists and in the churches themselves it is possible to discern four main strands of methodology in contemporary church-based education.

Four Main Approaches
4.8 **An Instructional Approach**

It is clear that in many congregations across the denominational spectrum in Britain and Ireland the legacy of practice in recent centuries is evident in the continuing preference for an instructional approach to teaching ' the faith handed down'. This somewhat misnamed `traditionalist' approach begins with the disciplines of knowledge. It is an informational model through which knowledge essential for the moral and spiritual well-being of the child is passed on from teacher to pupil. Despite the fact that the notion of learning by doing is as old as education itself, the heritage of our immediate past has bequeathed to us an approach based upon the notion that knowledge should lead to action rather than arise from it. Faith commitment was reckoned to result from an understanding of the content of faith as presented by the teacher.

Although there has been a considerable shift in educational theory in the churches over the past fifty years, it is obvious that in many places the practice is still one of a highly didactic, knowledge-driven approach. Contemporary syllabuses now in use among Sunday Schools and other church groups may offer much that is child-centred and activity-related, yet the mental set of those who teach remains often at the level of instruction and the reality is that the possession of information and the retention of knowledge are perceived as major criteria. The problems created by the persistence of such an attitude are exacerbated by the reality that many people's experience of children in church is limited to their own recollection of the Sunday School system of their own childhood.

4.9 The Experiential Approach

John Dewey wrote that `the child s own instincts and powers furnish the material and give the starting point for all education'. He saw also the need for the child's experiences to be so organized as to enable reflection, insight and understanding. Experience does not inevitably give rise to knowing, but experience that is carefully guided is the basis of effective education. In contemporary church curricula used in our congregations the programmes usually assume an experiential approach. `From experience, through experience, to experience' is a well-known dictum. In congregational programmes this takes the form of an activity-based approach with much connection-making between human experience and the insights and concepts of the faith found in the Bible and in tradition. This amounts to rather more than just starting `where they are'. It affirms that experience itself is the teacher and vehicle for communicating God's truth and influence. Practical methods range from the formal to the informal across a spectrum of activity in which imagination, discussion, reflection, story and artistic self-expression are all important. In well-organized groups the methodology can be elaborate and the investment of resources most impressive. Even so, the results do not always match expectations.

4.10 The Community as Educator

As noted earlier, the faith community has a vital part to play in the education and nurture of those within its sphere of influence. Where the Church as the people of God lives out what it believes, the possibilities for building up faith in individuals and in the group are awesome. It is in the community of believers, in its life, rites and rituals, activities and worship that faith is found, developed and owned. Because the possibilities for learning are rooted in the community itself, there is a growing tendency to explore and develop strategies whereby people of all ages are encouraged to learn together. Although the patterns of learning range from all-age Sunday School to inter-generational learning and worship, sometimes using liturgical models, the essential insights hold good. Learning together is both a means of strengthening the community and of enhancing the faith experience of the individual. Children have something to bring to the learning group from their own experiences and perceptions which, when shared, benefit and inform the whole group. In the true community of faith all have something to learn and each has something to give.

4.11 Learning as Liberation

Focus on a theology of the Kingdom of God which calls for liberation from oppression, whatever form this takes, and which promotes justice and peace is a crucial component in any serious contemporary attempt to develop children or adults in the Christian life. Following the seminal influence of the work of Paulo Freire in `conscientizing' impoverished people in Brazil to the oppressive social realities of their existence, and the emergence of a vast literature on liberation theology, the attention of Christian education has turned increasingly toward `humanization'. In this respect the work of Thomas Groome in North America has attracted much attention and interest. Groome has developed an approach to the faith tradition which takes account of interactions between an individual, the learning group and the situation in which they find themselves.

Experience and action are followed by reflection, which leads on to further action. Thomas Groome describes this approach as `Shared Praxis'. The shared praxis approach has many applications and holds much promise for further development, especially in terms of envisioning God's purpose for his people and of target-setting for specific action and discipleship.

4.12 Another area of investigation to develop over the past two decades, and one of great interest to those engaged in the Christian nurture of children and young people, centres on the spirituality of children. The insights of the Religious Experience Research Unit based in Oxford, under the leadership of Edward Robinson, merited much interest and stimulated further research. By analysing the accounts of childhood experiences recounted in later life by many adults, Robinson concluded that a child has a picture of human existence peculiar to him/herself which can so easily be forgotten - what he termed `the original vision'. The experiences associated with it are essentially religious. He concluded that childhood is not just a chronological period of human development but a continuing and influential element of the whole person. `In childhood we may be wiser than we know.'

4.13 Any consideration of the process of faith development is incomplete and inadequate without frank and full acknowledgement of the possibility and increasingly common reality of the faith journey that is arrested or abandoned. A moment's reflection on the statistical trends in the mainstream churches is sufficient to bring home the sorry truth of declining numbers in the Church in these islands. There are fewer people attending church, fewer communicants, fewer confirmations and fewer baptisms compared with twenty years ago. Among children in Sunday Schools and other church groups and organizations the problem of declining numbers is acute. This can no doubt be accounted for in large measure in terms of the social changes which have brought about what has been described earlier as `the erosion of childhood'. Even so, the churches should ask themselves just how seriously they have taken the paramount question of the nurture of children. With the first publication of *The Child in the Church* came the message, `the child is the Church of today'. This message quickly assumed the nature of a slogan in Church committees. What is less clear is the extent to which it became the basis for policy and practice in local

41

congregations. One reason for the failure of the churches to hold young people has been the inability and even the unreadiness of their adult members to make a place for children and teenagers within congregational life. The Church's concern for children is by no means restricted to those affiliated to the institution. The second of two influential Church of England reports on ministry among children, *All God's Children? - Children's Evangelism in Crisis*, expressed concern over the Church's perceived role towards the 85% of children who do not go to church or associate with it and for whom the major influences in terms of religion will be the home and the school. The comment: `It only takes two generations to de-Christianize a nation' is both arresting and challenging.

A Church Rejected by the Young

4.14 Attention to a deeper understanding of the processes of Christian nurture in general, and faith development in particular, will help us to understand the dynamics of rejection. We need to come to a fuller estimate of why it is that young people abandon the Church, its ideas and beliefs, its lifestyle and subculture. Many see it as an irrelevant failure. Is it the Gospel or the institution that they abandon? Contemporary theories of nurture, of which Westerhoff's is a prime example, focus on *nurture for decision.* These acknowledge a process of critical openness, of discourse between the individual and the Church. At appropriate times in the life-cycle, choices will be made with regard to the Church and the faith to which it testifies. Of the four styles of faith identified by Westerhoff experienced faith, affiliated faith, searching faith and owned faith it is the third faith style that deserves particular attention when considering why young people reject the Church.

It must be acknowledged frankly that congregations in the main have not been particularly good at enabling young people to question the values, beliefs and activities of the Church. It seems almost as though while it is acceptable for children to be given a sense of belonging in the congregation and so have experience of faith, however unexamined, and while they may be encouraged to affiliate to the life of the congregation by joining in the worship and other activities of the church, and while it is hoped for and prayed for that these same children will progress to the point of making personal commitments in faith, yet there is a nervous reluctance to encourage any form of doubt or questioning. If our young people do not have our `permission' to doubt, to ask, to probe and search and test the claims of the Gospel, then we must consider the realism of our approach. The questioning or searching style of faith is a necessary antecedent to owned faith. Young people need `space' in which to examine the gospel and its relevance for today. Too often their intolerance' of much within the institutional Church stems from a perceived discouragement to explore in an open-minded way the basic tenets of biblical faith and the doctrinal traditions of the Church. The search for meaning in life remains an essential quest for young people today. It is important that they should be encouraged to engage on this search from within the household of faith. To this end Christian nurture is a process requiring patience, love and a non-patronizing appreciation of the young person's quest for faith, meaning and identity within the frame of reference which the Church at its best is so wonderfully able to provide.

4.15 Young people live in a world of confusion in which conflicting signals are received about what is important and what is unimportant, about what is acceptable behaviour and what is unacceptable, about what is harmful or destructive and what is not. They have to come to terms with a system of values often characterized more by inconsistency and nonconformity than anything else. This applies to such basic standards as always speaking the truth, the appropriation of possessions, the use and abuse of natural resources and concern for the environment, the sustaining of relationships, the coming to terms with one's own sexuality and the assuming of responsibility for the general well-being of others and oneself. In the eyes of the young the world does not always practise what it preaches and, for that matter, neither does the Church. Such confusion is compounded by the cognitive dissonance experienced by young people as they attempt to bridge the gap between *propositions* they are expected to accept and their own inner *feelings* about the subject matter of these propositions.

The formation of attitudes is a highly sensitive area of nurture and one which must necessarily involve young people in a degree of experimentation with ideas and trial-and-error learning. Their quest is all the more difficult in an age in which there is a blurring of the boundaries between the world of the child and the world of the adult. Increasingly, and especially in the sphere of leisure, our young people are to be seen as `adult-children' interacting with `child-adults', that is to say with those of mature years who have not realized their potential in terms of personal maturation. This is a breeding ground for much uncertainty over values, standards and beliefs and one which requires to be addressed by the claims of the Christian gospel. Perhaps for too long we have relied upon a method that expects the adoption of Christian beliefs to issue in right behaviour.Perhaps there is more hope of success through an approach which commends `right behaviour' in terms of a Christian lifestyle which in its turn, and by its efficacy as a fulfilling way to live, will inculcate in the young person an acceptance of basic Christian beliefs.

4.16 In connection with the search for meaning on the part of young people, the Church may do well to pay greater heed to what might be termed *vocational dissonance*. This is the conflict and distance between ideals, visions and potential on the one hand and actual limited achievements on the other. This may be evidenced in under-achievements in terms of career, academic studies, sport or even in the realms of building relationships, and where failure leads to premature withdrawal from any encounter or engagement. There may be good reason for the Church to recover an adequate theology of vocation in which true fulfilment may be conceived as the courageous and adventurous response to the call to discipleship. It is perfectly possible for young people to recognize the validity of the spiritual   life in the Spirit   and the possibilities that this offers, yet to reject a Church that is judged to have failed and with it the God of the Church, branded as `the God that failed'. Perhaps these forms of dissonance are also part of the searching process. Yet they call in question the Church that would seek to recruit to its ranks the up and coming generation but only on the terms of those adults already secure within the Church. The nurture process is double-edged. It not only responds to the very question, `How shall we prepare our young people for Church?' It is required to take with the greatest possible seriousness the question `How shall we prepare the Church for our young people?' In plain language: what do we have to offer?

4.17 Children and young people need help in working through the searching periods in their lives. Too many churches, keen on receiving those who have `worked things through' and come to some measure of personalized or owned faith, leave to their own devices those who continue to toil and struggle. Yet are there not among older children and younger teenagers visionaries whose very idealism speaks a prophetic word to the Church? The Church needs to take seriously the journey of faith, the processes whereby individuals develop and progress, and the significance of the stages and phases through which they pass. While the Church has one eye on the potential of the young person, what he or she might become in the future, it must have the other eye on the actuality of what he or she is now, a child or young teenager to be accepted, affirmed and listened to. Just as the child is encouraged to be open to the Church, so the Church is called to be open to the child.

Children in the Community of Faith

4.18 If we are to take seriously the possibility of children *in* the Church, then a child-centred approach to Christian nurture is not fully adequate. Christian nurture has its locus in the faith community. Effective nurture is possible only where there is an appropriate environment and where there is a system of support. Congregations need to heed the warnings that the preparation of children for life in the Church may come to nothing unless they are prepared to receive and accommodate them and to meet the needs of the young.

4.19 There is urgent need in our congregations for a `whole-church' approach to development and education, children, youth and adults together. This in itself constitutes the basis for a massive programme of awareness education and reorientation of policy and practice in many congregations. Congregational development seeks to establish a vibrant, active faith community at the core of the congregation which will work to widen its sphere of influence throughout the congregation as a whole and to deepen the faith, understanding and commitment, the witness and service of those engaged in the life of the church, whatever their age, whatever their stage on the journey of faith. This requires of the local church vision, careful planning and good management. Above all, it requires a sense of wholeness, togetherness, a commitment to mutual support and the cherishing of a distinctive corporate identity. From such characteristics there emerges the confidence to be the Church and the faith to accomplish great things. In a word, we need in our congregations a sense of *koinonia*.

Transitions and Transformations

4.20 It would be quite wrong to portray human development including faith development as a smooth, trouble-free process of ascendancy from one level of being to a higher and more noble level. There are likely to be periods of crisis, trauma, setback, doubt, regression, personal confusion and disarray. Yet through these times of crisis the Gospel is conveyed through the message and life of the faith community. It is able to offer support, comfort, encouragement and strength to the individual - child or adult - in such times of difficulty and transition. A basic means whereby individuals and communities work through crises and problem situations is by recourse to ritual behaviour. This is true both in society at large and in the Church. Communities have ways of coming to terms with grief, sorrow, leaving home to enter into marriage, disengaging from the community, relocating the family elsewhere, breaking accepted codes of conduct, healing, change of status in the group, the birth of a child, the introduction of the child into the life of the community, and in due course into active or adult life. The `marking' of such processes of change, or *transitions*, in the lives of individuals are paralleled by the acknowledgement of transitions in the life of the community. These may relate to seasons or special group events. In primitive societies virtually all transitions are facilitated by rites of passage. Not all transitions in modern society are marked in this way. It may even be that the departure from or loss of rites of passage in secular society adds to the confusion experienced by individuals, not least by children, as they journey through life.

In the Church there is evidence of the same confusion where it adheres to rites which are no longer associated with any transitional experience and so have lost their meaning. Equally there are significant transitions through which people journey for which the Church has no rite of passage, for instance: starting school, getting engaged to be married, retirement. It may be that the recovery of the significance of rites of passage, a new understanding of the dynamics of the transitions facilitated by these rites and a reconsideration of the place and importance of ritual in modern society are matters to which the churches should give greater consideration.

4.21 In any consideration of the individual's journey of faith there is this caveat to be added. The faith journey is characterized not just by transitions but also, and fundamentally, by *transformations*. To be addressed by the Gospel of Jesus Christ is to face up to the possibility of radical change, the *metanoia* or shift of direction that transforms the values, perceptions, attitudes and commitments that express the core of human personality in such a way as to bring about a fundamental reorientation of the person around the reality of God in Jesus Christ. Such basic life changes need to be given expression within the context of the faith community which gave rise to them in the first place. This possibility raises questions about the level of expectation our congregations have of our young people coming to a personal commitment and owned faith. Ritual, rite and liturgy are capable of providing both the nurturing and evangelizing means of assisting people on the journey of faith, sometimes leading them progressively forward and at other times presenting them with the challenge to take decisions. It would be a grave error to reduce either the process of nurture or the dynamics of a faithful congregation to sociological description. Whatever rituals, rites, liturgies or rubrics the churches may contrive, they are but the vehicle for advancing God's purpose in drawing his people to himself. In the faith community God is at work and, ultimately, the faith that is professed in childhood, adolescence or adulthood is a gift of God and the fruit of his Spirit.

4.22 To the gift of faith we may add the gift of children. In all that goes before and in what follows there is a key assumption, that children are a gift from God. Children remind us of God's grace and that we are God's children by virtue of God's acceptance of us and not through our own efforts, talents, success, wisdom or learning. The presence of children within the Church causes us to articulate our Christian identity. Because we have to tell the children, we have to remember our significant stories, and explain our worship and our life. The questions which children both ask and pose demand responses. As these responses are formulated we can see that children have a role as teachers and agents of renewal and reformation.

4.23 Both in the Church and in the world children demand our love and care and draw us into responsible and selfless action. When we ask if either the Church or the world is a fit place for children, we not only judge ourselves but also find a standard by which to shape our vision. What is fit for children is fit for everyone.

Moreover, our caring for children enables us to reach a deeper understanding of God. When we know what it is to delight in particular children, to share their joys and comfort their sorrows, to find the balance between guiding their way and leaving them free, we begin to understand what we are saying when we speak of God as mother or father.

4.24 In all its endeavours the Church seeks to assist the children's passage in the life of faith, accepting them at all times as belonging within and as part of the Church of today. They are on a journey and it is our privilege, responsibility and vocation to journey part of the way with them. Tomorrow belongs to them. It is our task to encourage and nurture them in a Christian faith that will equip them for the new day. It will help us in our task if we have a fuller and deeper understanding of what it means for us to be the Church and it is to that possibility we now turn.

5 WAYS OF LOOKING AT THE CHURCH

5.1 A Method of Working.

There is a rich variety of biblical and theological resources to enable us to develop a well-grounded vision of how churches might relate to children. To consider these is to move away from a narrow view which sees children as empty vessels into which adults pour Christian knowledge. More than ever the churches need to stand in that place where the challenge of the scriptures and the experience of children within and without the churches will enrich our theology and reshape our practice. The church which in this sense takes children seriously will be transformed and will play its part in the transformation of the world. However, this process is not accessible to many Christians unless examples are made available.

5.2 What follows is not a systematic biblical or theological exposition. It is an exploration of six models or images of the Church, drawn from both old and new sources. Like a model of the solar system they are not the reality but a way of handling ideas so that they can be explored. All the models draw on biblical imagery, though in different ways. Different churches and individuals have different approaches to scripture. The approach adopted here is to draw on scripture as a source of inspiration and illustration, indicating the wealth of tradition available to the Church.

5.3 The six models of the Church used are:

> The new creation
>
> The Body of Christ
>
> The spirit-filled community - *koinonia*
>
> The pilgrim people
>
> The hospitable space
>
> The child

The models are not fully developed; they are, as it were, sketch maps rather than the ordnance survey. Not every model will have the same significance for each denomination or congregation. Even within a single church the meaning may vary at different times. It is hoped that the models have a potential for congregational development both by being challenging and by enabling people to express their own ideas. Both the challenging and enabling are important. Having enabled the Church to develop its thinking and grow in understanding is of little value unless it results, sooner or later, in significant action.

5.4 The New Creation

The first model is grounded in the God who makes and remakes the world and all that is in it. It puts forward a vision and a hope which finds expression in a variety of ways - whether as the Kingdom .of God preached and exemplified by Jesus, the new creation taught by Paul, or the vision of the Holy City, the new Jerusalem. In Zechariah's vision of the new Jerusalem old and young live in truth and righteousness and the streets of the city are full of boys and girls playing (Zechariah 8.1-8). Jesus taught that God's generosity shows the futility of human anxiety (Matthew 6.25-34). In 2 Corinthians 3, 4 and 5, Paul shares his vision of how the new covenant in Christ leads to a new creation, both of individuals and the world itself. Similarly, he uses the picture of the whole created universe groaning with the pangs of childbirth as a result of God's action in Christ (Romans 8). The new Jerusalem in John's vision is a place where the wealth and splendour of the nations is sanctified and all the people of earth healed because God's new order has been completed (Revelation 21, 22).

5.5 The God who is known in this model is one who seeks justice for all and who calls people to become involved in making the vision a reality. God's promise becomes true when its truth is lived. It is a challenge to the Church to become a community which demonstrates both corporately, and in the lives of individual Christians, the quality and character of the redeemed life which is lived in loving response to God's love. The life of the individual Christian and the local church is given a context within the global mission of God, bringing freedom and new life to all. In recent years the churches have recognized the links, both practical and theological, between justice, peace and the integrity of creation. These issues, which are already reflected in the concerns of children as well as adults, will be crucial in the next decades. The churches will need both to demonstrate and encourage ways of living which are just, peaceful and sustainable.

5.6 For churches and individuals there is a tension between the already-given and the not-yet- possessed Kingdom of God. There is a need both to recognize and rejoice that true justice, peace and harmony are God's gift to the world through Christ and also to struggle to attain them. Too much emphasis on the gift can lead to complacency and an abdication of responsibility; too much emphasis on the struggle risks the dangers of over-busyness and impatience. All Christians are called to find the right balance between grace and response, to find in the tension the point of personal transformation where they can become channels for God's creativity in the world.

5.7 When things go wrong in creation it is the weak and vulnerable who bear the burden. Very often these are children. The effects of social disease are magnified in their lives. Our lack of love and justice is apparent in their poverty. It is children who are most often the voiceless and the powerless. Yet children are also symbols of hope; they point us to a better future. At the very point of their need the transforming God offers us a glimpse of the new creation. The challenge for the Church is not only to read the signs in the lives of children but to let children speak for themselves. In the new creation the voiceless find a voice; the powerless lay hands on the levers of power. How is that to happen for children in the churches and more generally in society?

5.8 A church with this model will reflect the tension between `the already and the not yet'. Conflict and struggle within a church are, however, usually experienced as negative rather than as the pangs of new creation. This is because we have not learned to accept the gift of God's justice, peace and harmony. If we have grasped that security we are not afraid to explore difference. Action will bring the tensions to the surface. Working with people raises social and political questions. This is why we often stop at a discussion of the new creation rather than trying to co-operate in God's creative work. Trying to address the needs of children in society transfers to the life of the congregation some of the tension which children experience in their lives and it may be uncomfortable.

5.9 If the local congregation is conservative or complacent the understanding of new creation cannot simply be overlaid on existing thinking. It demands a new commitment arising from a dissatisfaction with what exists. When people ask the Spirit of the living God to take them, shape, mould and fill them with new life, they have all too often set limits beforehand. The new creation model of the Church speaks to the radical edge of the Gospel. When the churches have lost direct contact with so many children and young people it may be that radicalism is inescapable. As the understanding of the Gospel is recreated, so the institutional structures of the Church are called in question.

5.10 **The Body of Christ**

This model draws on the image of the body which Paul develops, for example, in 1 Corinthians 12. Paul says that no part of the body is unimportant. In the body of Christ no one can say to another `I do not need you' nor can anyone say of himself or herself, `I do not belong'. If one part of the body suffers, all suffer. For the purpose of this model it is assumed that children within the Church are part of the body of Christ. It is recognized that not all churches would agree with this and, furthermore, that those churches which would agree often act as if they do not. When we affirm that children are part of the Body of Christ we have to consider the implications. Paul writes of the gifts given by the Holy Spirit to the church through individuals and of the ministries which enable the Church to function as one body. Taking this model, children have both gifts of the Spirit and ministries to exercise. It may be in this context, rather than in baptismal debate, that we need to take the text of Mark 9.37: `Whoever receives one of these children in my name receives me' (*New English Bible*).

5.11 Children can have a ministry which represents Christ to the Church, reminding people of the incarnation and embodying the weakness which God chose. They can have a distinctive priestly ministry, representing all children within the church and its worship. They can have a distinctive teaching ministry in which they ask apparently innocent questions, voicing the doubts and questions which adults are too self-conscious to raise and enabling answers to be found for all. They can have a distinctive prophetic ministry when they notice our failure to live by the gospel we proclaim and ask us why. They can have a distinctive ministry in worship, not as entertainers, but calling us to share all that is holy and rich in meaning for everyone rather than just the preoccupations of the middle- aged.

5.12 Children have a ministry beyond the church community. They may act as evangelists amongst their friends or families. Many parents have been drawn to Christian commitment through their children. Children may have an apostolic ministry in being sent out to the places where children are, making Christ present in the world. Within the playground they may work against bullying and racism, befriend the lonely or show a generosity of spirit, all of which make the Spirit of Christ evident to other children.

5.13 A church with this model will find ways to recognize and receive ministries from children. The issue to be considered is whether an acceptance of children as part of the body of Christ is a sentimental gesture or whether it has real substance. The local congregation can simply add children's events to its programme or treat children as substitute adults. Because the children of the churches do not fit into the adult structures of government and planning they are likely to be excluded from participation as definitively as the house-bound. Those who are most in contact with them may also be least involved in the overall organization of a congregation. It is not simply a question of structures and representation but one of ethos and mind-set. If there is a will to take the ministry of children and the ministry among children seriously, ways can be found of drawing on their insights and energies. This will not always be comfortable, for when the ministry of children is acknowledged it can be seen that through it God challenges the structures of authority within the Church. Nor is it a case of shifting inappropriate responsibility to children; the task is to discover how children and adults together can encourage and support one another in carrying out the implications of faith in their daily lives and how together they can sustain that faith in worship, prayer and study.

5.14 The Spirit-filled Community - *Koinonia*

Koinonia is a word used in the New Testament to describe the life of the early Church, e.g. Acts 2.42. It is difficult to translate into English but its meaning includes community, communion, participation, sharing and fellowship. *Koinonia* is also used for the activity of the Holy Spirit within the Church, for instance in 2 Corinthians 13.14. As churches have developed this concept they have also seen *koinonia* as describing interpersonal relationships within the Trinity, the divine giving and receiving which is the fountain and life-giving source of all human forms of fellowship. So to say that the Church is a community in the sense of *koinonia* is to say more than that it is a collection of people assembled together. It is a community of faith, filled with the Spirit of the risen Christ, in union with God and all God's people, as described, for instance, in Ephesians chapters 1-4.

5.15 It is the Holy Spirit which draws the community together and empowers it. At Pentecost the Spirit gave power to prophesy, which was bestowed on all, both young and old, and the courage to make open proclamation of the Gospel (Acts 2.4ff). The Spirit drew the Church together in the sharing of food and possessions (Acts 2.44-46). In the Gospel of John the gift of the Holy Spirit is accompanied by the power of forgiveness (John 20.22-23). Jesus described the Spirit as leading to truth (John 16.13). It is the presence of the Spirit in power which enables the enlargement of the Church to include Gentiles (Acts 10.44-48). The Spirit not only makes the Church one, it also makes it dynamic.

5.16 How is *koinonia* to be identified? What does it mean to be a spirit-filled community? One sign is equality, which is symbolized for most churches in a common baptism, the same for everyone, regardless of social status, wealth or gender (Galatians 3.28). Another sign is sharing, not only within the Church but with those outside. In most churches this is symbolized by the offering and sharing of bread and wine at the Eucharist. The symbolism of baptism and Eucharist means more than equality and sharing. Some Christians exhibit the signs without the sacraments; but *koinonia* will be evident in ethos as well as action. A third and related sign is forgiveness, symbolized in many churches by the formal exchange of the peace. Jesus taught that forgiveness should precede common worship (Mark 11.25, Matthew 5.23-24). A forgiving and forgiven church will be a community of reconciliation and mutual acceptance and a place of healing.

5.17 A fourth sign is truth, both in the willingness of a Christian fellowship to search for ever greater understanding of God's purpose and in the integrity between word and action demonstrated by believers. A fifth sign is prophecy, the prophetic vision which sees the world through the eyes of God. It knows the world as it is and the world as it could be and proclaims both judgment and mercy. Two more signs come from the teaching of Jesus. The first is his command to love one another (John 13.34); to love one's neighbour (Mark 12.31); and to love one's enemy (Matthew 5.44). The second is his saying that his family, mother, brother and sisters are those who do the will of God (Mark 3.31-35). The Spirit-filled community is recognized by the quality of its life shown in acts of love and obedience to God and neighbour.

5.18 Within the faith community, people discover the meaning of who they are, both individually and corporately, through such things as relationships, worship, symbolism, celebration and story. All these serve to shape, and to continue shaping, their faith and life. Through these kinds of activities the continuity of the community is secured from generation to generation; through them children learn their identity and are helped to discover and develop their faith. As the story of faith is retold to a new generation, the power to transform both hearer and teller may be rediscovered and the Church brought back to the origins of its life. When children ask `Why do we do these things?' they challenge the Church to articulate its Christian identity and recreate the excitement of the discovery of the power of God.

5.19 Outside the faith community *koinonia* cannot be separated from *diakonia*, which may be translated `service'. The bread to be shared must not remain purely symbolic but become real in practical generosity. The Christian community is committed to a just sharing of the world's resources. This leads to a simple lifestyle; conspicuous consumption cannot be right when others are in want. The Christian community must extend its practice of equality, forgiveness, truthfulness and love to the wider world, with all the consequences for social and political action which follow. Bringing all children within the ambit of these concerns may pose serious questions about the priorities of the Spirit-filled community.

5.20 A church with this model will be a place where faith and discipleship are intertwined and lived out. It will tell its story in teaching and worship in such a way that its relevance to life and action is clear. It will find ways to encourage faithful Christian living. In such a church the adults will set an example for children to follow and they will make a point of initiating them into the meaning of worship and other church activities. They will also make it clear that it is the one Spirit which generates community within every congregation. Christians, including Christian children, need to anchor their Christian identity in a particular household of faith. But they also need to know that there is an overall identity as Christ's people. In some places, only by co-operating can congregations offer service to children. In others they need to find ways of expressing their overall identity in concrete ways for children. Not every denomination needs its own playgroup or advice centre. Specialist services, such as support for parents, may use pooled resources. Children, within and without the churches, need to see that discipleship is located in both an immediate fellowship and a wider common confession.

5.21 The Pilgrim People

The idea of a pilgrim people as a model of the Church is based on two biblical images. The first of these is found in the story of the Exodus and the wilderness experience of the people of Israel. This image suggests a dynamic model of people on the move who have left their old life behind and are journeying to a distant promised goal. On the journey they discover who God is, their own identity as a people of God, and how they can live together. This model is hopeful but realistic; it recognizes that the way is long, the people grow disheartened and not all will make the journey. It is a model, too, which stresses faith and dependence on God, who feeds the people in the wilderness, provides for their needs and gives the sign to be followed on the way. The second image is that of 'the way', the name used for the early Church before they were called Christians (e.g. Acts 24. 14,22). The whole writing of Luke includes an exploration of this theme, with the Gospel itself journeying from Galilee to Jerusalem (Luke 9.51-19.27) and from Jerusalem to the ends of the earth (Acts 1.8). Similarly, in Mark's Gospel the way is a metaphor for discipleship. Jesus goes before on the way (Mark 10.32). He calls his friends to take up their cross and follow him (Mark 8.34). The way brings its own dangers and surprises. On the way to Emmaus the risen Christ walks unrecognized by his two friends while teaching them the significance of what they had experienced (Luke 24.13f).

5.22 Within this model the Church and individual Christians are seen

as being on a journey of faith. The experience and tradition of the past may help to guide the way but much of the future is unknown except to hope. There is the possibility of creative and exciting movement but also of back-tracking. There will be wrong turnings and places of crisis where decisions are difficult. At times there will be oases of rest. However, the caravan must move on and face the challenge of the desert again. As the community makes its journey it will encounter others on the way. Some will join it; some will share the journey for a while before going on a different route. Some members will scout ahead, discovering distant vistas and speaking of what they have seen as they return. Some members will be far behind, perhaps encumbered with the accumulated baggage of the years, and the rest of the community must wait in patience for their slower pace to bring them on, perhaps helping them with the weight of their load. Whatever happens the community cannot stop; without the journey it has no purpose. It is driven to change and go forward, however difficult it may be. At its best a pilgrim Church knows its tradition and its significance sufficiently well to be able to move on with confidence, making new meaning consonant with old.

5.23 To this Church children bring their gift of visible growth and change, helping everyone to remember that all are on the journey. Children may well be those who explore ahead and alongside the path, stopping sometimes to call attention to the wonder of something new to them, though familiar to adults, and asking questions about the journey and its purpose. Where are we going and why? In attempting the answer to those questions adults may rediscover their own sense of excitement and wonder and realize that they are still journeying themselves. They induct the children into the disciplines of mutual help and respect which make the journey possible. Children are trusted with part of the load which has to be carried and taught to look out for one another.

5.24 A church with this model will expect to change and takes risks. It will be able to give an account of its vision and its hope. It will deal lovingly with those who are burdened with fearfulness but it will not let fear deflect it from its path. It will enjoy the journeying and celebrate its arrival points. It will not be afraid to turn back, especially when the going is easy, to return to the path which has been pioneered by Christ. It will learn from every step, every encounter and every mistake. It will share its experience with other groups of pilgrims on the road.

5.25 Risk-taking is not something we commonly associate with our ministry to children. We go to extra lengths to ensure their safety throughout church activities. Yet in the sense of which we speak of pilgrimage here it is taken for granted. Children expect new experience and change against a background of stable relationships. Their voice needs to be heard in shaping future plans. How far are they consulted when a congregation says to itself `We need to do something more for children'? They will have the same mix of ignorance and insight as the adult members but different ways of expressing it. They may be so used to being `done to' that it will take time to build their confidence to make suggestions. The simple business of asking children for their views is not in itself risky. It is more difficult to find out what they think, rather than what they think you want to hear. Trusting their insight and judgement may call for even more vision and courage. As in so much of what is said here the test is whether, having accepted the rhetoric of the ministry of children, we are ready to be led by them.

5.26 The Hospitable Space

Throughout the gospels when Jesus tells stories about the Kingdom he uses the image of generous hospitality at a feast. Those who are ungracious enough to refuse invitations are replaced by others (Luke 14.15-24). The Kingdom has room for social misfits and aliens (Matthew 8.11,12). Jesus himself was hospitable, even in a lonely place, and fed the hungry crowd, organizing them in manageable groups so that the space and atmosphere was created for a meal in which all were generously fed (Mark 6.39,40). He built on the generosity and hospitality of others, so that the child's loaves and fishes, once offered, were more than enough (John 6.1-13). He accepted hospitality at Bethany, in the house of Martha, Mary and Lazarus and elsewhere. He invited himself to those who were thought unworthy to be his host (Luke 19.1-10). The feeding miracles appear to be connected with both the feast of the Kingdom and the Last Supper, where the Passover meal is given new significance in the Christian tradition. The risen Christ ate with his friends, teaching them, accepting their doubts and allowing them the opportunity to put questions (Luke 24.36ff). Apart from the deeper significance of many of these events, they testify to an awareness that real learning takes place with human encounter and that the hospitable table puts people at their ease and allows them to learn from one another.

5.27 In this model the Church is a place of hospitality and nurture. It receives hospitality from Christ, who is himself the host, drawing the lost to himself with loving acceptance and offering to share the bread of life with all. In the spirit of Christ the Church itself offers hospitality with courtesy and gentleness and with unconditional love. It accepts people for what they are and celebrates all that is good in them and all that they may become. It provides a safe space, both physical, psychological and spiritual, within which they can question and grow. To be a place of welcome it must be a place of forgiveness; to be true to itself it must be a place of hope and transformation. For this to happen it cannot afford to be guided only by sentiment. A hospitable community is a place where love confronts as well as forgives. In order to. offer tolerance, forgiveness and affirmation it must also be honest and mutually accountable. Hospitality can be abused. Making a place hospitable for the vulnerable, especially children, means adopting proper safeguards. It is one thing to be open to risk; it is another thing to court disaster.

5.28 To this Church children bring two gifts. The first is the gift of their own needs. Children need to be made welcome and to feel accepted. They need a safe place where they can play, learn, grow, question, challenge and be challenged. They need to be nurtured and celebrated, even when they are at their most awkward and unlikeable. Their need for a safe and welcoming community is a gift to everyone because the church which can rise to this challenge has begun to make itself a hospitable space for adults as well. Children's second gift is that of friendship. They can make friends across age groups. They make opportunities for adults to communicate with each other. Their presence helps to create a sense of mutual dependence. This gift, too, calls on the whole church to make itself into a hospitable space for a whole range of other people.

5.29 A church with this model will pay attention both to the attitudes and practices of its community and also to the physical building, which may testify to its values far more than what is said or written about it. In some churches there is a particular bond between the young and the old. It is as if each feels marginalized by the active and busy parts of the congregation and takes delight in each other's company. Each has time to talk to the other after worship. Each may have thought of some token of friendship to bring and share. Each encourages the other. It is a sad indictment of our churches if the `hospitable space' is confined to these groups and we have not learnt from them and shared their gifts. We all need others to have time for us and to slow ourselves down for long 'enough to have time and space for other people.

Adjusting the physical space of a church with sensitivity to the needs of children and the elderly is only the beginning. If a church strikes children as an uncaring or hostile place, why should it be any different for adults? We may have strategies to cope with the strains of church life, or an adult ability to internalize our difficulties, but is that the kind of discipleship to which we are called? Whatever else these models may offer congregations, we hope that this notion of an open and accepting community will be taken seriously.

5.30 The Child

This model is grounded in the words of Jesus, `The Kingdom of God belongs to such as these: truly I tell you, whoever does not accept the Kingdom of God like a child will never enter it' (Mark.10.14-15, *Revised English Bible*). These words provide the Church with both the puzzle and the challenge of what Jesus meant when he directed his followers to accept the kingdom like children. The Church has to give serious consideration to what it means to be as a child. It can be seen as being full of potential; it is not yet all that it might be. On the other hand, what we think of as an unformed state may in itself be what is acceptable to God. In the gospel context of teaching about discipleship the child is seen as powerless, as one who is unable to withstand the barriers raised by the authority of the disciples. The child has been brought into the midst when the disciples were disputing about authority (Mark 9.33-37). In this, as in the calls to be without power of possessions and money, the values of the gospel are in direct contrast with the values of the world (Mark 10.21-25).

5.31 The particular gift of children is to provide the living reality which gives meaning to this model. Many of the qualities of individual children may not be helpful, but that will prevent the Church from reaching too easy and too sentimental a conclusion about what is demanded. Rather than thinking of the children the Church would not want to be like, it is possible to isolate the gifts of childhood. Being a child is not a choice of weakness or passivity but is a way of interacting with others and responding to the world.

5.32 The Church as a child is dependent on God, receiving grace and blessings as a gift and living in trust. It follows God in faith, not counting the cost, for God has already paid the price. Viewed as a young child it tries to be like its parent and to do what the parent does; viewed as an older child it feels safe to explore rebellion and questions. Like the child at play it is imaginative, inquisitive and spontaneous. It experiments, reshaping and reconfiguring the world, delighting in what it finds. It is prepared to look from new angles, to use things for new purposes, to turn the world upside-down. It has no choice but to be powerless, to refuse the world's weapons, whether psychological, economic or military. It imposes its will on no one and does not resist force with force but with the weapons of the Spirit: truth, love and peace. The Church as a child is adventurous and active, learning through what it does. It is not always limited by caution. It enjoys and celebrates life for its own sake rather than with some end or purpose in mind.

5.33 A church with this model would live by the values of the Kingdom. It would risk its property, if it had any, on adventures of the Spirit. It would count its pennies without any real anxiety for its long-term finance. It would be considered exasperating and irresponsible by some and refreshing by others. It might often be in trouble with someone but it would consider it more important to be right with God. It would be light of heart and tenacious of purpose, a community of rejoicing and a community of resistance. It would be generous to people beyond its own immediate circle. It would accept people from a wide range of cultures in an unselfconscious way. The worship of such a church would be very imaginative and allow room for spontaneity. The wider Church would enjoy its support and confidence and it would be ready to receive advice and help from outside itself. People would want to belong to it because of its ethos rather than its organization. There would be respect for others without pomposity and a capacity to build on history rather than to be its prisoner.

5.34 Challenge to the Churches

The purpose of these models has not been to offer a blueprint for the Church but to test different ways of looking at it. They will be most helpful if they encourage churches to find their own models, their own ways of working and of being communities of the gospel. What has been done here is to take ways of thinking about the Church and test them against the needs and gifts of children. This both develops a vision of what the life of the Church might be and raises very serious questions for the churches. These are questions which, in effect, children are asking by their very presence. How do adults listen to children and, having listened, do they take any notice of what they say? Which ministries of children are recognized and how are they encouraged to exercise them? What stories are important enough to be shared with children and how are they exemplified in the lives of adults? What is being done to make the Church a friendly and safe place for children and how are they shown that they are welcome? What are the values of the Kingdom and how are they lived in the world?

5.35 Similarly searching questions might be asked of the children in churches. Who can they talk to in their church and what would they want to say? What do they do at church which is important to them and how are they helped to do it? What do they know about why their church is there and what questions do they want to ask? Who can they make friends with at church and who could they befriend? How does their coming to church help them in their life at home and school?

5.36 If, instead of trying to teach good news to children, the Church tries to *become* good news, it will need such fresh eyes to see itself. Such a Church would have the confidence to deal with questions rather than always having to find the answers. It would be prepared to surrender its life and let its institutions be transformed. The sadness is that churches rarely have the confidence which enables them to face the questions theology may ask of them, especially in the devastating directness such questions take on in the mouth of a child. Churches lack the humility to face the truth about the quality of their life and worship and to set about addressing the needs which are then identified. A Church which welcomes children, accepts their gifts and ministries, meets their needs, advocates justice, seeks new life, challenges evil with love and truth, and continues to learn the values of the Kingdom by living them, is a Church which is good news not only for its members but for the world.

6 GOOD PRACTICE

Building on Good Practice

6.1   In applying the models described in the previous chapter, the churches bring with them a significant amount of valuable experience. Although there are many ways in which the churches have failed to take children seriously, there is much that is good in attitude and activity which can provide a starting point for development. This chapter attempts to identify actual examples of good practice which should be affirmed.

6.2   What are described are only examples. This is not an exhaustive list of all that is good. Readers are encouraged to reflect on what they would count from their own experience and observation as good practice.

6.3   The examples are offered as descriptions of ways of thinking and acting which embody the values advocated in this report. They are not examples in the sense that readers are being encouraged to replicate them exactly. Rather it is hoped that readers will take encouragement to work appropriately in their own situations.

Examples of Good Practice
National

6.4   The government minister welcomes the representatives of the churches who have come to express their concern about the effect of proposed legislation on children. They have prepared carefully so that their arguments are not easily dismissed.

6.5   A group of adults are meeting in a conference centre. From the accents it is possible to detect that there are people from Wales, Scotland, Northern Ireland, the Republic of Ireland and England. From the discussion, these are church people with a concern for children. They are the CCBI Consultative Group on Ministry among Children. They represent the wide range of Christian traditions in membership with the CCBI. Some are full-time officers of their churches, others are members of boards and committees. It is out of this commitment to each other and to children that there has come the original *Child in the Church* report and this document.

6.6   The *Children's Charter* began as an attempt within the United Reformed Church to raise issues about the place of children in the Church. It has been taken up and reproduced by many different denominations and agencies.

6.7 It was the first time children had ever been on the agenda of the Deanery Synod. Members had been asked to discuss the Church of England report *Children in the Way* as part of a national process of consultation and awareness raising. As they read the report, they discovered that there were some serious issues to consider. As they discussed they found themselves not only asking questions concerning what to `do about' children but also about themselves as adult Christians and about the whole life of their parishes.

Regional

6.8 Members of school governing bodies and boards are gathering together from across the area. In addition to that function they have one other thing in common: they are all members of the different churches in the area. They are meeting together to consider what the resources of Christian faith offer to the challenges which confront their schools and to offer one another mutual support and encouragement.

6.9 The cathedral is crowded with children who move in groups from one workshop to another. They are exploring a theme through art, drama, mime, craft, music and prayer. The bishop is leading one of the workshops. The final act of worship includes aspects of each workshop.

6.10 Children from all the main Christian traditions come with their leaders for a weekend at the Corrymeela Centre for Reconciliation to explore the theme `A Walk Through Holy Week', using activity-based learning.

6.11 The Baptist Association has drawn children and adults from across three counties for an all-age celebration of faith. They have prepared for the evening's worship in mixed age workshops.

Local

6.12 The children push their way noisily into the church hall. Some of them still have plenty of energy left at the end of the school day. Others have had enough and want some peace and quiet. The after school club with its games, art stories and open spaces offers opportunity for both needs to be met. The church building is safe and familiar territory to the children. Many of them first came in a pram to the mother and toddler group and then graduated to the play group before moving into school. As early evening comes, the children leave one by one as parents pick them up on their way home from work.

6.13 They prepare you for giving birth in ante-natal classes but no one prepares you to be a parent. This has been a godsend.' This is the parenting group held in the church lounge. The initial fears of those attending that it might be the vicar telling them what to do and giving unrealistic expectations of family life have not been realized. Through using the Family Caring Trust's *What Can a Parent Do?*, they have been able to share experiences and help one another.

6.14 After morning worship, children and adults climbed on to the double-decker bus they had hired and drove into the countryside. They were glad that it was a sunny day but their experience last year told them that even heavy rain would not ruin the day. There was no planned programme - only to enjoy being together. They picnicked on the field beside the village church. Some played games in the afternoon, whilst others sat around chatting, or explored the area. Before going home children and adults shared in an act of worship in the church.

6.15 The church members of an inner-city congregation decide to use their resources to help break the relationship between social deprivation and low educational attainment. They organize and staff a homework club for children living in the area.

6.16 It was not what some would call a proper orchestra. It only consisted of the instruments which happened to be played by people in the church. Some people weren't too confident, like the girl who had just learnt the recorder and the man who had to search for his French Horn in the attic. Others were able to give a lead, like the teenager who had just passed grade 8 on the violin. By working together and with a careful choice of music, they were able to make a creative contribution to the worship of the church.

6.17 The children sat quietly, staring intently at the priest standing at the altar. Something in the action, something in the atmosphere had caught them up. It didn't matter that they couldn't understand every word or explain everything that was happening. It all felt so mysteriously important and they felt glad to be there.

6.18 The discussion had started when someone in the church meeting questioned why the church supported charities like NCH Action for Children and Barnardos. Weren't they out of date in a modern welfare state? No one could answer so the church secretary was asked to write away for information. At the next church meeting, there was considerable surprise at the information available and shock at what it told them about the life of children today. As a result, donations to `good causes' became part of the mission of the church.

6.19 Groups of children and adults are meeting in different rooms and corners of the church premises. All are considering the same aspect of faith, they are all drawing on and valuing their own experience of life, the Church and God as well as drawing on the resources that the Christian faith offers. For all of them, learning is about doing as well as listening. It is also about prayer and worship.

6.20 The leaders and teachers had joined the training group because they wanted to learn better ways to do their work with children. As they worked together, using the *Kaleidoscope* training material, they began to reflect on their own faith and to ask some searching questions about the part they played in the total work of their church. They found a new awareness of their faith as well as practical skills. In sharing the sessions with leaders from neighbouring churches, they discovered common concerns and opportunities.

6.21 The primary school to be built in the middle of the large green-field housing development was to be a Church school in replacement for an elderly building on the main road. The vicar called a meeting of ministers and representatives of the two other churches in the old part of the town to consider how the new Church school could become a focus of community activity and a worship centre sponsored by all the churches. They agreed that the new Church school should become part of the mission strategy of all the churches working together.

6.22 There was nowhere suitable for divorced or separated parents to spend time maintaining their relationship with the children to whom they had access. That was until the church decided to use its premises as a contact centre.

6.23 The Church Council were discussing arrangements for worship over the Christmas period. They had heard some ideas which had been put forward by the (adult) congregation and thought of ways of involving various people in preparing the worship. The question was raised, `What shall we do with the children?'.

'Well, we've consulted everyone else and involved them in preparing. So why not the children too?' The Church Council agreed. After Christmas everyone knew that in future the children should always be consulted and involved.

6.24 One church decided to refurbish the room used by a children's group. When the children themselves learnt about this and the amount of money which was to be spent, they renegotiated the arrangement. The children's real concern was not with the shabbiness of their room but the poverty of children in India. They worked with the adults in re-painting the room and turned down the offer of new furniture. At their insistence, the cash released was sent to OXFAM.

6.25 The family fearing the deportation of the father took refuge in the church. It made the members of the church unpopular with the authorities and a few individuals locally. As well as keeping a family together, offering sanctuary forged new links of trust with the local community.

6.26 Quakers remember stories from the seventeenth century. When Quaker meetings were illegal and adult Friends were put in prison, the children, despite threats from the authorities, kept the public meetings for worship going. Even though there was no one over sixteen present, these were still recognized as fully authorized meetings for worship.

6.27 Everyone recognized that the entrance to the church was not very welcoming. Children in the church were asked to design welcoming posters. Some children each week were also invited to join the adults in greeting worshippers to the Sunday morning service. People remarked on how welcoming the church was. The children said they began to feel that it was 'their' church.

6.28 The arts festival centred on church premises brought together children of different races and faiths. In enjoying each other's company, new relationships were formed. In talking together mutual understanding grew.

6.29 Members of the church had been expressing concern about the children of the area. The feeling that the church ought to be doing something was so strong that an open meeting was organized. As the evening went on they discovered that the church was already active - in the congregation they had teachers and ancillary staff in local schools, parents who went into school to help with reading and other projects, people who worked in the police force and social services. No one had noticed this before and the church had not affirmed or helped them in their 'ministry'. This set a new agenda for the church.

Drawing Together the Threads of Good Practice

6.30 What links the examples above is that they are all concerned with the response of the community of faith to children. Their diversity is a reminder that there is no single blueprint for the churches in relation to children.

6.31 To some, the examples offered will be commonplace. The quality of the ordinary and everyday is just as important, if not more so, than high profile 'state of the art' schemes.

6.32 Good practice is never perfect practice. In all the examples above there are aspects which do not meet the ideal or there is room for improvement. If the descriptions are read critically, it should be with a view to improving what is done, rather than knocking other people's work.

6.33 The fact that there are many examples of good practice, both those recorded here others, should not make the churches complacent. There is much unfinished business. One thread running through this report is that there are valid insights which were expressed in reports such as *The Child in the Church* which have not yet informed our thinking. Another is that society has changed dramatically for children. These demand a change in our attitude to children as well as in our activity with and for children.

6.34 The examples indicate that there are many answers to the questions 'What kind of people do we need to be?' and 'What should we do?' Such answers will be a response in and through faith. They must also be appropriate to and arising from the people concerned and their situation. They will be shaped by the theological models by which the Church works. Churches have often been limited in their relationship with children by adopting only one model of working and not keeping that under review. Chapter 5 has offered a range of models which, in various combinations, may become appropriate in particular places and times. Too much bad practice has occurred because churches try to apply concepts and methods inappropriately and insensitively.

6.35 Good practice will demand that the churches work ecumenically. There are strong arguments for this from the point of view of the good use of resources. The churches are more likely to be heard as an advocate for children if they speak with one voice. The principal demand for an ecumenical response is God's undifferentiated love for children.

6.36 Good practice is not simply a by-product of Christian faith, it is integral to it. All that the churches are and do should be grounded in the love of God in Jesus Christ reconciling and healing a broken world.

6.37 It is not enough for the churches to be concerned about attracting children to worship or to the organizations they run. God demands, and children deserve, more than that. In the past, churches and Christian individuals have taken risks in the use of their resources and with their public popularity in acting for and with children. The churches today are called to take new risks and to change in attitude and activity towards and with children in a faithful response to God.

RECOMMENDATIONS

It has been assumed in these recommendations that churches will act together, wherever possible, in the spirit of the Lund principle. This is the basis of all work in the Consultative Group on Ministry Among Children.

L = local action, R = regional or district action, N = national action

The numbers after each recommendation refer to paragraphs in the Report.

Children and Families

1 Depending on local circumstances, churches should consider whether to provide facilities for the following groups to meet on church premises and find volunteers to assist in their running:

   (a) play groups 1.4, 1.14f, 2.7f, 3.11f, 6.12

   (b) parent and baby groups 1.6f, 2.7f

   (c) divorced parents with access to children 1.8, 6.22 (L)

2 Churches should offer regular opportunities for parents to reflect on their role and to take up programmes of training. 2.7f, 6.13 (L)

3 Churches should make provision at a local level, for the support and development of volunteers who work with play-groups, parent and toddler groups, or training in parenthood. (R,N)

4 Churches should secure resources from public funds and from appropriate agencies to sustain the systematic training and support of volunteers working with parents and children. (R,N)

Christian Development and Formation

5 Churches should review their arrangements for training and supporting those around whom the nurture of children within the congregation is focused. The review should take into account the increasing reluctance of adults to commit themselves to traditional `children's work'. 2.16, 2.23f (L,R,N)

6 Churches should reconsider the terminology used in an integrated, whole-churchapproach to Christian education. This may require the conscious abandoning of the language of `school' and `teacher' applied solely to the learning activities of children. 2.15f, 2.23f (L,R,N)

7 The preparation of programmes for work with children should be informed by the best possible professional advice on the ways in

71

which children learn and, in particular, how they learn about God. 2.6, 2.23, 2.32, 3.5, 4.5f (L,R,N)

8 The churches of Britain and Ireland together, or acting together through their national instruments, should promote a post or posts devoted to research into religious learning among children and the further development of the discipline of Christian education for all ages in the church setting, as distinct from religious education in schools. Any such post should be located in an appropriate institution of higher education. 4.5 (N)

9 For the purposes of following the recommendations in this section churches should arrive at a definition of childhood as they understand it, differentiated from adolescence and youth, and describe its characteristics. This definition should be the reference point in implementing the recommendations in this report so far as children are concerned. 2.16 (L,R,N)

Children and Society

10 Churches should secure better information about the position of children in society as a whole. 2.1f (L,R,N)

11 Churches should press for better co-ordination of public policy in matters affecting children. 1.9, 1.13, 1.14, 1.21, 1.22, 1.25, 2.2, 3.4, 3.9, 3.12, 3.15f, 5.8, 6.4 (L,R,N)

12 Churches should be aware of the work of local social services with children and offer appropriate support. 2.1f, 5.33, 6.24(L)

13 Churches should cultivate models of life-styles which contrast with those which promote consumerism. 2.3, 5.20, 5.33 (L,R,N)

14 Education against prejudice should be a specific component of church programmes of work with children. 1.13, 1.22f (L,R,N)

15 On behalf of the churches an individual or working group should undertake a systematic theological study of our understanding of childhood today and publish a report. 2.17, 4.22f (N)

Children and Church Organisation

16 Churches should review the assumptions which lie behind the activities which they organize for children and ensure that they take into account the varying needs of children and their place in contemporary society. 2.15f, 2.23f, 4.8f, 4.14f, 4.18f, 5.13, 5.20, 5.25, 5.29, 5.33, 6 (L,R,N)

17 Churches should include a specific reference to children in any systematic review of their mission or response to calls for evangelism. 2.29f, 4.17, 5.9, 5.12, 5.25, 5.36 (L,R,N)

18 Churches are encouraged to examine their self-understanding by reflecting on the Bible and Christian doctrine in the manner of chapter 5. (L, R, N)

19 Churches should monitor their educational materials and policy statements with a view to ensuring that they address the needs of people across society and are not making narrow assumptions based on class. They should also pay attention to issues of equality, which are reflected in the statements and policies of most other public bodies. 2.4, 2.28 (N)

20 Churches should ensure that the formal pre- or post-ordination programmes of study for clergy and ministers include a consideration of how children are best served by the churches and how their gifts can be best used within them. 2.15f, 4.14f, 4.18f, 5.1, 6.7 (N)

21 Churches should co-operate in carrying out an enquiry into the specific reasons for rejecting church life or Christian belief given by young people who have grown up in the church community and in publishing the results. 2.15, 4.13, 4.14f (N)

22 The design of new and refurbished church buildings should take into account the need of churches to provide what is here termed `hospitable space' 5.26f (N, R, L)

23 Churches should ensure that all activities organized for children conform with the terms of current legislation affecting children. (L, R, N)

Children and Worship

24 Churches should encourage the development of family celebrations and rituals which make explicit the faith and values which are implicit in Christian family life. 2.11 (L,R,N)

25 Churches should offer families the opportunity to celebrate and recognize significant moments in their life. One aim of this would be to give children a sense of continuity and roots. 2.21, 2.22, 4.20 (L)

26 Churches should take care that their selection of liturgical material and the implicit assumptions of their corporate life affirm the value of every child in their diversity of family backgrounds. 2.4, 2.28 (L,R,N)

27 Churches engaged in the publication of liturgical materials should ensure that they are appropriate for the diversity within worshipping congregations; this should not be taken to mean that

materials are to be `written down' to children. 2.4, 2.20, 2.22, 2.28, 4.4, 5.20, 5.26, 6.9, 6.11, 6.17, 6.23 (N)

Churches and Schools

28 Churches which have not undertaken a role as providers of schools should review their position in the light of the changes towards a secular ethos in education which have taken place over the last fifty years. This review should be conducted in partnership with churches which are providers. 3.15f, 3.27 (R,N)

29 Churches should seek to be supportive of schools in their locality and to co-operate with them, where possible, in offering pupils experience of Christian life and worship, and in the development of spirituality across the curriculum. 3.20, 3.23 (L)

30 Churches should offer personal support to Christians who are teachers and encourage the vocation to teach. 3.21f (L,R,N)

31 A thorough review should be made of the experience of chaplaincy in non- denominational schools and national policy agreed. 3.24 (N)

32 The churches should clarify their theological understanding of education. 3.7, 3.17 (L,R,N)

BOOKLIST

Reports and other material produced by the CGMC:

Bible and Children, The British Council of Churches 1988

Child in the Church, The British Council of Churches 1976

Children and Holy Communion British Council of Churches 1989

Kaleidoscope (training material) National Christian Education Council 1993

Understanding Christian Nurture British Council of Churches 1981

Other publications:

Aboud, Frances *Children and Prejudice* Basil Blackwell 1988

Aries, Phillipe *Centuries of childhood* (English translation by Robert Baldick) Jonathan Cape 1973

All God's Children? National Society/Church House Publishing 1991

Armstrong H *Taking Care* National Children's Bureau 1991

Astley J *The Philosophy of Christian Religious Education* Gracewing 1994

Astley J (ed) *How Faith Grows* National Society/Church House Publishing 1991

Astley J and Day D *The Contours of Christian Education* McCrimmon 1992

Astley J and Francis L (eds) *Christian Perspectives on Faith Development* Gracewing 1992

Bax J *Finding God Today* Darton Longman and Todd 1990

Bernstein E and Brooks-Leonard J *Children in the Assembly of the Church* Liturgy Training Publications 1992

Bradshaw J *Child Poverty and Deprivation in the UK* National Children's Bureau 1990

Bridger F *Children Finding Faith* Scripture Union 1988

Brown K and Sokol F C *Issues in the Christian Initiation of Children* Liturgy Training Publications 1989

Butler P *Reaching Children* Scripture Union 1992

Children in the Way National Society/Church House Publishing 1988

Coles R *The Spiritual Life of Children* Harper Collins 1992

Copsey K *Become Like a Child* Scripture Union 1994

Crawford K *Under 5s Welcome* Scripture Union 1990

Cully I V *Christian Child Development* Gill and Macmillan 1980

Cully I V *Stages of Faith: The Psychology of Human Development and the Quest for Meaning* Harper Collins 1981

DeMause L (ed) *The History of Childhood* Psychohistory Press, New York 1974

Duggan R D and Kelly M A *The Christian Initiation of Children* Paulist Press 1991

Fowler J *Stages of Faith* Harper & Row 1976

Fowler J *Weaving the New Creation* Harper Collins 1991

Fowler J, Schweitzer F and Nipkow K *Stages of Faith and Religious Development* SCM Press 1992

Francis L *Making Contact* Collins 1986

Frank P *Children and Evangelism* Marshall Pickering 1992

Gobbel R & G *The Bible - A Child's Playground* SCM 1986

Grassi J A *Children's Liberation: A Biblical Perspective* The Liturgical Press, Minnesota 1991

Graystone P *Help! There's a Child in my Church* Scripture Union 1989

Graystone P and Turner E *A Church for All Ages* Scripture Union 1993

Groome T *Christian Religious Education* Harper & Row 1980

Groome T *Shared Faith* Harper & Row 1993

Hay D *Exploring Inner Space* Penguin 1982

Hay D *Religious Experience Today* Mowbray 1990

Hull J *What Prevents Christian Adults from Learning* SCM Press 1985

Hull J *God-talk with Young Children* Christian Education Movement 1991

Hull J (ed) *New Directions in Religious Education* Falmer Press 1982

Hull J (ed) *Studies in Religion and Education* Falmer Press 1984

Jenkins D and Thornton S *Children of the Wilderness* United Reformed Church 1989

Kellmer Pringle M *The Needs of Children* Hutchinson 1985

Kumar V *Poverty and Inequality in the UK* National Children's Bureau 1993

Magdalen Sr *Children in the Church Today* St Vladimir's Seminary 1991

Ng D and Thomas V *Children in the Worshipping Community* John Knox, Atlanta 1981

On the Way Church House Publishing 1995

Orchard S (ed) *The Pursuit of Truth in Community* Christian Education Movement 1992

Pearson G *Save our Children* Grove Books 1993

Postman N *The Disappearance of Childhood: How TV is changing children's lives* Comet 1985

Postman N *Amusing Ourselves to Death* Heinemann 1986

Pritchard G W *Offering the Gospel to Children* Cowley Publications 1992

Pugh G *Contemporary Issues in the Early Years* National Children's Bureau 1992

Purnell P *Our Faith Story* Collins 1985

Quinn M *How to Hand on Faith to your Children* Fowler Wright 1993

Religious and Moral Education 5-14 Scottish Consultative Council on the Curriculum 1992

Religious Education: Model Syllabuses Schools Curriculum and Assessment Authority 1994

Rummery G and Lundy D *Growing into Faith* Darton Longman and Todd 1982

Saris W *Living the Faith Together* Collins 1985

Saris W *Towards a Living Church* Collins 1985

Stone M K *Don't Just Do Something - Sit There* Quaker Home Service 1992

Sutcliffe J *Learning and Teaching Together* Chester House Publications 1980

Sutcliffe J *Learning Community* National Christian Education Council 1974

Van Ness P *Transforming Bible Study with Children* Abingdon Press 1991

Walker L *All is Gift* Collins 1987

Weber H R *Jesus and the Children* World Council of Churches 1979

Westerhoff J *Bringing Children up in the Christian Faith* Winston Press 1980

Westerhoff J *Building God's People in a Materialistic Society* Seabury Press 1985

Westerhoff J *Learning Through Liturgy* Seabury Press 1978

Westerhoff J *Will Our Children Have Faith?* Seabury Press 1973

Westerhoff J and Willimon W *Liturgy and Learning Through the Life Cycle* Seabury Press 1980

Working With Children in the Church National Christian Education Council 1988

Churches and Bodies Affiliated to the CGMC

Baptist Union of Great Britain
Christian Aid
Christian Education Movement
Church of England
Church of Ireland
Church of Scotland
Church in Wales
Churches' Commission on Mission - Junior Education Group
Congregational Federation
Council for Sunday Schools and Christian Education in Wales
Independent Methodist Churches - Young People's Department
Irish Methodist Department of Youth and Children's Work
Methodist Church
National Christian Education Council
New Testament Assembly
New Testament Church of God
Presbyterian Church of Wales
Religious Society of Friends
Roman Catholic Church
Salvation Army
Scottish Sunday School Union
Sunday School Society for Ireland
United Reformed Church
Welsh National Centre for Religious Education
Westhill College